EFFECTIVE STRATEGIC LEADERSHIP

Educated at St. Paul's School, John Adair has enjoyed a varied and colourful career. He served in the Arab Legion, worked as a deckhand on an Arctic trawler and had a spell as an orderly in a hospital operating theatre. After Cambridge he became Senior Lecturer in Military History and Leadership Training Adviser at the Royal Military Academy, Sandhurst, before becoming Director of Studies at St. George's House in Windsor Castle and then Associate Director of The Industrial Society.

In 1979 John became the world's first university Professor of Leadership Studies at the University of Surrey. He holds the degrees of Master of Arts from Cambridge University, Master of Letters from Oxford University and Doctor of Philosophy from London University, and he also is a Fellow of the Royal Historical Society.

In 2006 the People's Republic of China conferred on John the title of Honorary Professor of Leadership Studies in recognition of his 'outstanding research and contribution in the field of Leadership'. In 2009 the United Nations appointed him Chair of Strategic Leadership Studies at its central college in Turin.

www.johnadair.co.uk

EFFECTIVE STRATEGIC LEADERSHIP

THE COMPLETE GUIDE TO STRATEGIC MANAGEMENT

JOHN ADAIR

PAN BOOKS

First published 2002 by Macmillan

This edition published 2010 by Pan Books
an imprint of Pan Macmillan, a division of Macmillan Publishers Limited
Pan Macmillan, 20 New Wharf Road, London N1 9RR
Basingstoke and Oxford
Associated companies throughout the world
www.panmacmillan.com

ISBN 978-0-330-50943-5

Copyright © John Adair 2002, 2010

The right of John Adair to be identified as the
author of this work has been asserted by him in accordance
with the Copyright, Designs and Patents Act 1988.

Typeset by SetSystems Ltd, Saffron Walden, Essex
Printed and bound in the UK by
CPI Group (UK) Ltd, Croydon, CR0 4YY

Visit **www.panmacmillan.com** to read more about all our books
and to buy them. You will also find features, author interviews and
news of any author events, and you can sign up for e-newsletters
so that you're always first to hear about our new releases.

CONTENTS

FOREWORD

It is a real pleasure to welcome you to this book. While fully revising *Effective Strategic Leadership* for this second edition I was reminded of what fun it was to write it in the first place. So I do hope that you will not only profit from these pages but also enjoy the time you spend reading them.

Publishers understandably tend to measure the success of a book by the number of copies it sells, while for their part academics count the number of citations by colleagues in journals or conferences. Neither of these particular success criteria speaks to me. The success or failure of this book in your hands for me relates directly to its aim, which is to enable *you* to become a more effective strategic leader. We are partners in that common enterprise, each with our part to play.

You have the hardest part, for you have to *do* strategic leadership. My contribution is to stimulate your thinking, to equip you with some well-tested frameworks and to get you started on your journey. If you return occasionally to these pages in the course of your career and find inspiration and renewed hope, then this book will have served you well.

John Adair

INTRODUCTION

There is a widespread sense that across the world – whether in industry and commerce, the public services, government or the voluntary sector – there are not enough really effective strategic leaders, at least not in the numbers required. This shortfall is actually a global phenomenon.

A strategic leader is essentially the leader of an organization. An *effective* strategic leader is one who delivers the goods in terms of what an organization naturally expects from its leadership in times of change.

This book is written primarily for those who aspire to become effective strategic leaders. You may already be head of an organization, or know that you are next in line for such a role, or you may simply be aware that the path of your vocation is leading you in that direction.

That doesn't exhaust the list of those who can read this book with profit! In large organizations there is – or should be – a strategic leadership team working under the conductor's baton of the head person. Obviously the more each member knows of the principles and practice of strategic leadership, the better they can support and complement the contribution of their leader.

Do not assume, however, that this book only applies to those who work in large or medium-sized organizations. The body of knowledge and ideas it contains, especially the parts relating to strategic thinking, is equally relevant to those in charge of small organizations, and indeed to those like myself who work in unstructured fields. As the Roman playwright Plautus said: '*Ergomet sum mihi imperator*' – 'I am myself my own commander'. Today each of us has to be our own strategic leader.

Leading the way – whether for an organization or for yourself – is never easy. I hope that this book equips you for the challenge and that you enjoy reading it too.

The book is largely self-explanatory. Part One maps and explores the sources and fundamentals of strategic leadership – as far as I can tell for the first time. Part Two moves on to what you have to do today to be effective in the role, focusing on five key themes.

The idea that strategic leadership – *leading* your life – is a universal concept, one that is relevant to everyone, is so new that I doubt if this book will escape the fate of being classified, at least initially, as another management book. Yet there is material here for schools and universities as they gradually wake up to the challenge of helping young people to prepare for working life.

As with other books in the *Effective* series, I have given as many case studies and practical examples as possible to illustrate the principles. You can skip the material in boxes if you like, or return to it on a second reading. The summary of Key Points at the end of each chapter is designed as a succinct *aide-mémoire*, but occasionally I throw in a new idea just to see if you are still awake! I have spared you checklists, but you can easily ask yourself questions as you go along in order to relate what I am saying to your own situation.

To get the best out of a book like this one, however, you do need to widen your span of relevance. By that I mean that we naturally look for examples or case studies in our own field, such as business or education, and deem these to be relevant. But to see relevance in the examples of say, an orchestral conductor or a Greek general to leading a company or a school does call for what I call a *wide span of relevance*. It is the same principle, incidentally, that lies behind creative thinking – the sparks of meaning jump between two or more apparently unconnected things to produce new ideas.

For my assumption is that there is an underlying unity in strategic leadership, whatever field you are in and however structured or unstructured your work in it may be. When you study effective strategic leaders in organizations or as individual contributors for yourself, encouraged I hope by these pages, you will be increasingly aware of how much they have in common. Therefore you can draw lessons and insights from many sources in order to grow as a strategic leader.

> *There are many paths to the top of the mountain*
> *But the view is always the same.*
>
> Chinese proverb

PART ONE

UNDERSTANDING STRATEGIC LEADERSHIP

1

THE WORLD'S FIRST THOUGHTS

'Those having torches will pass them on to others.'

Plato

Words are sometimes like nuts: if you crack them open you discover the kernel of their meaning. *Strategy* is a case in point. It is made up of two ancient Greek words. The first part comes from *stratos*, which means an army spread out or a large body of people. The second party, *egy*, comes from the Greek verb to lead. There is a rough breathing mark in the Greek that explains the spelling of the English word *hegemony*, meaning the leadership one nation or group of nations exercises over another or others, which is derived from it.

It was Athens, rivalled only by Sparta, which claimed the hegemony of the Greek city-states. Around 500 B. C. a senior commander in the Athenian army came to be called a *strategos*, leader of the army. The English word we use to translate this word is *general*. It literally means something or someone that or who is applicable to the whole. So a military general is accountable for the whole army as well as its parts.

In the Athenian citizen army during the fifth century B. C., there were ten large units based on the old tribal strands in the city. Later in Athenian history these units were commanded by what we would call professional soldiers but in the early days the ten *strategoi* were elected by their fellow citizens. To get elected a *strategos* was an important step on the political ladder for any ambitious young Athenian. Great leaders of the city-state such as Themistocles and Pericles had arisen by this very route. But the need for election acted as a hurdle: how could one get one's fellow citizens – the voters – to vote in one's favour? One man seems to have thought about this question – Socrates.

SOCRATES 'THE THINKER'

We tend to think of Socrates as an old man but he was only about thirty-five years old when he began to be well known in Athens. By then he had served as a *hoplite* – a fully armed spearman – in at least three campaigns and carried himself with distinction. Indeed his courage and even heroism in battle became legendary. The gifted but wayward young general Alcibiades tell us, for example, that during a siege on the north Aegean coast Socrates saved his life when he was wounded and beset by enemies. He also remarked upon his friend's remarkable indifference to the bitter winter conditions, wearing his ordinary thin clothing and going barefoot in the snow.

The small group of young men who gathered around Socrates like moths at a lamp were drawn by both his remarkable intelligence and his personality. One of these 'Socratics' was Plato, who said of his master: 'Of all men whom we met at that time, he was the wisest, most just, and the best.' What sort of man did they see? In middle age Socrates presented an unusual appearance. It was said he had a head like a *satyr* (in Greek mythology, a male, wood-roaming companion of Pan and Dionysius, often depicted on Attic painted vases with a goat-like aspect) complete with snub-nose, wide nostrils, protruding eyes and thick lips. Other descriptions also give him a paunch. He wore simple threadbare clothes and still walked barefoot but now with a peculiar limping gait. This was the man they nicknamed 'The Thinker'.

The son of a stonemason, Socrates constantly drew the analogy between the skills of artisans and craftsmen – the physician, the leather seller, the metalworker – and the wider roles and responsibilities of a citizen's life, indeed that very life itself. All these practical skills could be learned by careful analysis, education and training and, where necessary, by experience, as everyone agreed. Socrates always professed himself unable to understand why the higher or more difficult arts – political leadership, statesmanship and the administration of justice, for example – were not acknowledged to be susceptible of the same treatment. Instead, he observed, these jobs were handed over to mere charlatans (such as Thrasymachus the 'sophist' in Plato's *Republic*, demagogues like Cleon the leather seller and others of a similar kind described by the comic playwright Aristophanes and the historian Thucydides).

Socrates himself wrote no books. Our principal sources of information about him are the writings of two of his inner circle: Plato and Xenophon. As they both wrote their various works in the form of Socratic dialogues it is not easy to determine whether the voice we hear is that of Socrates on the one hand or of Plato and Xenophon on the other. But what is best called the situational theory of leadership – that in any situation people will tend to follow or obey the man or woman who knows what to do and how to do it – is found in both Plato and Xenophon and attributed to their master. It is a sound surmise that it goes back to Socrates himself. Both use the example of a ship's captain and his crew. Here is Plato's version from the *Republic*:

> The sailors are quarrelling over the control of the helm
> . . . they do not understand that the genuine navigator can
> only make himself fit to command a ship by studying the
> seasons of the year, sky stars and winds, and all that
> belongs to his craft; and they have no idea that along with
> the science of navigation, it is possible for him to gain, by
> instruction or practice, the skill to keep control of the
> helm whether some of them like it or not.

Encouraging others by confessing his own lack of knowledge, Socrates set out to think things through for himself in discussion. Thereby he led his interlocutors on a journey of the mind. Towards the end of it they began to see and discover for themselves what knowledge or skill was required in any human being. Socrates, essentially a philosopher, believed that knowledge is virtue and virtue knowledge – it is knowing the good and knowing how to seek it in any circumstance. For Plato, that journey would lead him ever further away from the practical issues of living and working that interested Socrates, far into the realm of abstract ideas, the domain of philosophy which would forever bear his stamp. But his fellow student, Xenophon, would take a very different course.

THE CASE OF THE YOUNG CAVALRY COMMANDER

One day, Xenophon tells us, Socrates engaged in discussion with a newly elected cavalry commander. As Xenophon himself was elected to that office it is tempting to believe that this is a piece of autobiography and he is describing here his first encounter with 'The Thinker'.

Under questioning from Socrates, the young man agreed that his seeking of the rank of commander could not have been because he wanted to be first in the cavalry charge, for, as Socrates pointed out, the mounted archers usually rode ahead of the commander into battle. Nor could it have been simply in order to get himself known by everyone – even madmen, he conceded, could achieve that. He accepted Socrates' suggestion that it must have been because he wanted to leave the Athenian cavalry in better condition than when he found it. Xenophon, both a renowned authority on horsemanship and the author of a textbook on commanding cavalry, had no difficulty in explaining what needed to be done to achieve that end. The young commander, for example, must improve the quality of the cavalry mounts; he must school new recruits – both horses and men – in equestrian skills and then teach the troopers their cavalry tactics. All these points emerged step by step out of the dialogue.

'And have you considered how to make the men obey you?' continued Socrates, 'Because without that, horses and men, however good and gallant, are of no use.'

'True, but what is the best way of encouraging them to obey, Socrates?' asked the young man.

'Well, I suppose you know that under all conditions human beings are most willing to obey those whom they believe to be the best. Thus in sickness they most readily obey the doctor, on board ship the pilot, on a farm the farmer, whom they think to be the most skilled in his business.'

'Yes, certainly,' said his student.

'Then it is likely that in horsemanship too, one who

clearly knows best what ought to be done will most easily gain the obedience of the others.'

Xenophon captures here that very distinct theme in Socrates' teaching on leadership already identified above. In harmony with the rest of his doctrine (for, despite his pose of ignorance, Socrates had ideas of his own), it emphasizes the importance of *knowledge* in leadership. People will obey willingly only those whom they perceive to be better qualified or more knowledgeable than themselves in a particular situation.

THE CASE OF THE ASPIRING GENERAL

One of the young Athenians around Socrates announced that he wished to stand in the annual election of ten generals in the city's army. Socrates encouraged him to attend the classes of an itinerant teacher called Dionysodorus, who had recently arrived in Athens and advertised a course in generalship. When the young man returned he had to endure some good-humoured banter from Socrates and his friends.

'Don't you think, gentlemen,' said Socrates, 'that our friend looks more "majestic", as Homer called Agamemnon, now that he has learned generalship? For just as he who has learned to play the harp is a harper even when he does not play, and he who has studied medicine is a doctor even though he does not practise, so our friend will be a general for ever, even if no one votes for him. But an ignoramus is neither general nor doctor, even if he gets every vote. Now,' he continued, turning to the young Athenian, 'in order that any one of us who may happen to command a regiment or company under you may have a better knowledge of warfare, tell us the first lesson in generalship Dionysodorus gave you.'

'The first was like the last,' the young man replied. 'He taught me tactics – nothing else.'

'But that is only a small part of generalship,' replied Socrates. By question-and-answer he then led the young man into a much fuller understanding of the knowledge and abilities required for a successful military leader. A general must be good at administration, so that the army is properly supplied with military equipment and provisions. Moreover, as Xenophon knew from his own experience, a general should ideally possess a number of personal qualities and skills:

> He must be resourceful, active, careful, hardy and quick-witted; he must be both gentle and brutal, at once straight-forward and designing, capable of both caution and surprise, lavish and rapacious, generous and mean, skilful in defence and attack, and there are many other qualifications, some natural, some acquired, that are necessary to one as a general.

Even on the all-important subject of tactics, Socrates found the instruction given to his young friend by Dionysodorus to be deficient. Did Dionysodorus give *no* advice on where and how to use each formation? Was *no* guidance given on when to modify deployments and tactics according to the needs of the many different kinds of situations one encounters in war? The young man insisted that this was the case. 'Then you must go and ask for your money back,' said Socrates. 'For if Dionysodorus knows the answer to these questions and has a conscience, he will be ashamed to send you home ill-taught.'

In this Socratic dialogue, as in the previous one, Xenophon is offering instruction in the art of being a strategic leader. What he is doing is helping his young listeners to form a complete *concept* of strategic leadership, in contrast to the limited or imperfect notion of it offered by Dionysodorus and his kind. The Socratic view is roughly that what prevents you from being a good leader is – in the first place – that you do not have a *true* concept of strategic leadership. If you could but *see* the truth, then you could hardly prevent yourself from moving towards it. Although neither Athens nor any of the other Greek cities had any business schools, the figure of the itinerant guru speaking to large audiences for fat fees on such subjects as the art of public speaking, generalship, or how to be happy and successful was a familiar one. These sophists, as they were called, were clever men, some more than others, known for their adroit, subtle, plausible reasoning but lacking in substance. Socrates and other philosophers regarded them as glib, superficial and out for money (Socrates himself did not charge fees).

Often, as in the case of Dionysodorus, the sophists did not really know what they were talking about. When Hannibal – arguably one of the ten greatest generals of all time – was in exile at the end of his long career, his host Antiochus, the Greek king of Syria, took him to hear a lecture by an elderly sophist who specialized in military leadership. 'Well, what did you think of it?' Antiochus inquired at the end. Hannibal looked at the king with his one remaining eye and replied in his characteristically dry, laconic, humorous way: 'In my time I have had to listen to some old fools, but this one beats them all!'

THE CASE OF NICOMACHIDES

Once, on seeing Nicomachides returning from the elections, Socrates asked him, 'Who have been chosen generals, Nicomachides?'

'Isn't it just like the Athenians?' Nicomachides replied. 'They have not chosen me after all the hard work I have done since I was called up, in the command of company or regiment, though I have been often wounded in action.' (Here he uncovered and showed his scars.) 'They have chosen Antisthenes, who has never served in a marching regiment nor distinguished himself in the cavalry and understands nothing but money-making.'

'Isn't that a recommendation,' said Socrates, 'supposing he proves capable of supplying the men's needs?'

'Why,' retorted Nicomachides, 'merchants are also capable of making money, but that doesn't make them fit to command an army!'

'But,' replied Socrates, 'Antisthenes also is eager for victory, and that is a good point in a general. Whenever he has been choirmaster, you know, his choir has always won.'

'No doubt,' conceded Nicomachides, 'but there is no analogy between the handling of a choir and of an army.'

'But you see,' said Socrates, 'though Antisthenes knows nothing about music or choir training, he showed himself capable of finding the best experts in these activities. And therefore if he finds out and prefers the best men in warfare as in choir training, it is likely that he will be victorious in that too; and probably he will be more ready to spend money on winning a battle with the whole state than on winning a choral competition with his tribe.'

'Do you mean to say, Socrates, that the man who succeeds with a chorus will also succeed with an army?'

'I mean that, whatever a man controls, if he knows what he wants and can get it he will be a good controller, whether he controls a chorus, an estate, a city or an army.'

'Really, Socrates,' cried Nicomachides, 'I should never have thought to hear you say that a good businessman would make a good general!'

By his familiar method of patient cross-examination, Socrates won agreement from Nicomachides that successful businessmen and generals perform much the same functions. Then Socrates proceeded to identify six of these functions or skills:

- Selecting the right man for the right job
- Punishing the bad and rewarding the good
- Winning the goodwill of those under them
- Attracting allies and helpers
- Keeping what they have gained
- Being strenuous and industrious in their own work

'All these are common to both,' Nicomachides accepted, 'but fighting is not.'

'But surely both are bound to find enemies?'

'Oh yes, they are.'

'Then is it not important for both to get the better of them?'

'Undoubtedly; but you don't say how business capacity will help when it comes to fighting.'

'That is just where it will be most helpful,' Socrates concluded. 'For the good businessman, through his knowledge that nothing profits or pays like a victory in the field, and nothing is so utterly unprofitable and entails such heavy loss as a defeat, will be eager to seek and avoid what leads to defeat, will be prompt to engage the enemy if he sees he is strong enough to win, and, above all, will avoid an engagement when he is not ready.'

The amazement expressed by Nicomachides at Socrates' line of argument in this dialogue rings true. For the teaching of Socrates, that people will only follow leaders who have the authority of knowledge relevant to a given situation, must have been well known in Athens. Moreover, in that city, businessmen were held in low social regard. Young gentlemen from good Athenian families would seek military and political careers, but they did not become merchants. Of course the scale of commerce and industry before the Industrial Revolution was relatively small and the scope for leadership was correspondingly limited. Armies and navies, by contrast, remained the largest and most important forms of common human enterprise until relatively recent times. In the mid-eighteenth century, for example, the Royal Navy of Great Britain was the largest industry in Western Europe.

Socrates did challenge this Athenian snobbery that has cast such a long shadow in history. 'Don't look down on businessmen, Nicomachides,' he said towards the end of their discussion. 'For the management of private concerns differs only in point of number from that of public affairs. In other respects they are much alike, and particularly in this, that neither can be carried on without men, and the men employed in private and public transactions are the same. For those who take charge of public affairs employ just the same men when they attend to their own; and those who do understand how to employ them are successful directors of public and private concerns, and those who do not, fail in both.'

AUTHORITY FLOWS TO THE ONE WHO KNOWS

Socrates, then, clearly taught that professional or technical competence should be a prerequisite for holding a position of leadership responsibility. Here Xenophon and Plato are doing more than handing on that torch to us. 'You must have noticed,' said Socrates, 'that a man who is incompetent does not attempt to exercise authority over our harpists, choristers, and dancers, nor over wrestlers. All who have authority over them can tell you where they learned their business.'

The tendency of people to follow a leader who knows what to do, observed Socrates, is strengthened in a time of crisis. In a discussion with Pericles, named after his father, the famous statesman, which took place when an army from the Greek state of Boeotia was threatening Athens, Socrates made the additional point that such a crisis should be more to an effective leader's liking than a period of ease and prosperity, for it is easier to make things happen. He illustrated this point with an analogy, the behaviour of sailors at sea:

> For confidence breeds carelessness, slackness, disobedience: fear makes men more attentive, more obedient, more amenable to discipline. The behaviour of sailors is a case in point. So long as they have nothing to fear, they are, I believe, an unruly lot, but when they expect a storm or an attack, they not only carry out all the orders, but watch in silence for the word of command like choristers.

In spite of his own military experience, which must have given him many opportunities to observe from the serried ranks of the Athenian phalanx of the competencies or incompetencies of the various generals he had served under, Socrates conducted these discussions on a general level, as befits a philosopher and teacher. But Xenophon was shortly to find himself in military command and faced with a real crisis. The teaching of Socrates would now be tested and shaped in the hot forge of experience.

Apparently against the advice of Socrates, Xenophon enlisted in a Greek mercenary army which the Persian prince Cyrus the Younger hired in a bid to replace his brother Artaxerxes II on the throne of Persia. In 401 B. C. a decisive battle was fought at Cunaxa, not far from ancient Babylon. The 10,400 Greek *hoplites* acquitted themselves well on the day, but Cyrus lost both the battle and his life.

After the battle of Cunaxa, the Persians offered the Ten Thousand (as the Greeks were later known) surrender terms if they stayed where they were but threatened to kill them all if they moved from their camp. In this crisis the man of authority was the most experienced of the six Greek generals – Clearchus the Spartan. He took the burden of decision upon himself.

Clearchus indicated that he would act as spokesman for his fellow generals to the Persian emissaries but gave no indication to anyone what he was going to say. After sunset he summoned a meeting of the officers, briefly reviewed the options and then told them what they must do. They must head northwards that very night on the first stage of a long march to safety on the shores of the Black Sea, which lay some 800 miles away. As Xenophon records in *The Persian Expedition*, everyone sensed that only Clearchus could lead them out of mortal danger:

> On receiving their instructions the generals and captains went away and carried them out; and from then on Clearchus was in command, and they were his subordinates. This was not the result of an election, but because they realized that he was the one man who had the right sort of mind for a commander, while the rest of them were inexperienced.

ARE KNOWLEDGE AND EXPERIENCE ENOUGH?

But is having knowledge and experience relevant to the situation – the general working field or the particular situation of crisis – the *whole* of leadership? Xenophon knew that it was not so. From his close observation of men in action, he made a distinction between those leaders who won *willing* obedience from their subordinates and colleagues, as compared to those who merely extracted compliance from them either out of fear or a grudging acceptance of the authority of knowledge.

Clearchus, the Spartan general who saved the day after Cunaxa, is a good example of such a limited leader. We can recognize men of his stamp again and again in military history. The Roman army depended upon men such as him. Their type would resurface in later armed forces: the Prussians of Frederick the Great, the British Royal Navy in Georgian times, the German *Wehrmacht* in the Second World War, and the American Army in Vietnam.

Clearchus was about fifty at the time of his death. He had spent much of his life at war, acquiring by hard experience a sound knowledge of his profession. But, as Xenophon noted, Clearchus never won the hearts of men. He had no followers who were there because of friendship or good feeling towards him. Xenophon continued:

> As for his great qualities as a soldier, they appear in the facts that he was fond of adventure, ready to lead an attack on the enemy by day or night, and that, when he was in an awkward position, he kept his head, as everyone agrees who was with him anywhere. It was said that he had all the qualities of leadership which a man of his sort could have.
>
> He had an outstanding ability for planning means by which an army could get supplies, and seeing that they appeared; and he was also well able to impress on those who were with him that Clearchus was a man to be obeyed. He achieved this result by his toughness. He had

a forbidding appearance and a harsh voice. His punishments were severe ones and were sometimes inflicted in anger, so that there were times when he was sorry himself for what he had done. With him punishment was a matter of principle, for he thought that any army without discipline was good for nothing; indeed, it is reported that he said that a soldier ought to be more frightened of his own commander than of the enemy if he was going to turn out one who could keep a good guard, or abstain from doing harm to his own side, or going into battle without second thoughts.

So it happened that in difficult positions the soldiers would give him complete confidence and wished for no one better. On these occasions, they said that his forbidding look seemed positively cheerful, and his toughness appeared as confidence in the face of the enemy, so that it was no longer toughness to them but something to make them feel safe. On the other hand, when the danger was over and there was a chance of going away to take service under someone else, many of them deserted him, since he was invariably tough and savage, so that the relations between his soldiers and him were like those of boys to a schoolmaster.

It is tempting to conclude that while Clearchus had great abilities as a soldier, and also as what we would now call a manager, he fell far short of being a great leader. One reason why people today often react so negatively to the idea of military leadership is because they assume that all military leaders are cast in the same mould as Clearchus. This is certainly not the case. Xenophon's last point, that Clearchus treated his soldiers like a *pedagogue* (literally in Greek a 'leader of children') is illuminating. The Greeks prided themselves on the belief that they were the most intelligent people on the face of the earth; they were deeply conscious, too, of their tradition of equality and democracy. They did not like being bullied or treated as children.

Xenophon, aged twenty-six, was elected as one of the successors to Clearchus and the other five Greek generals whom the Persians butchered in an act of treachery not long after Cunaxa. Having been taught leadership by Socrates, what style of leadership would Xenophon display? Doubtless he thought hard about that question. Obviously he did not want to be another Clearchus, nor did he want to err too far in the opposite direction of courting popularity and appearing weak. Xenophon tells us that Proxenus the Boeotian, one of the other murdered generals, had made that mistake. It was he, incidentally, who had first invited Xenophon to go on the Persian expedition, and so they were probably friends. Proxenus was a very ambitious young man and had spent much money on being educated by a celebrated teacher called Georgias of Leontini. 'After he had been with him for a time,' wrote Xenophon, 'he came to the conclusion that he was now capable of commanding an army and, if he became friends with the great, of doing them no less good than they did him; so he joined in this adventure planned by Cyrus, imagining that he would gain from it a great name, and great power, and plenty of money.' Yet, with all these ambitions, Proxenus made it clear to all that he wanted to acquire these things in a fair and honourable way or not at all. He liked to be liked, however, which led him into the mistake of appearing soft and of courting popularity for its own sake:

He was a good commander for people of a gentlemanly type, but he was not capable of impressing his soldiers with a feeling of respect or fear for him. Indeed, he showed more diffidence in front of his soldiers than his subordinates showed in front of him, and it was obvious that he was more afraid of being unpopular with his troops than his troops were afraid of disobeying his orders. He imagined that to be a good general, and to gain the name for being one, it was enough to give praise to those who did well and to withhold it from those who did badly. The result was that decent people in his entourage liked him, but unprincipled people undermined his position, since they thought he was easily managed. At the time of his death he was about thirty years old.

It could be said that Proxenus was not right for the military situation and could not establish the right relationship with his soldiers. But he would probably have been just as ineffective in non-military spheres of leadership as well. For Proxenus' very virtues created a certain lack of firmness or toughness which can lead to a loss of respect. Without respect, leadership is fatally impaired. A weak leader exposes himself to exploitation by his more unscrupulous subordinates. Bad leadership of this kind looks remarkably the same whatever the field or area of human enterprise.

Xenophon, who sat at the feet of Socrates, the Western world's first great teacher of leadership, now shows us what *he* meant by leadership.

A LEADER IN ACTION

Imagine yourself on a sun-baked, stony hillside on the southern edge of Kurdistan (on the borders of what is now Iraq and Turkey) watching this scene unfold before you. It is about noon; the sky is clear blue except for a line of white clouds almost motionless above a distant mountain range. Marching through these foothills come the advance guard of the Ten Thousand. The hot sun glints and sparkles on their spears, helmets and breastplates. They are hurrying forward, eager to reach the safety of the mountains in order to be rid of the Persian cavalry snapping like hunting dogs at their heels. But first they have to cut their way through the Carduci, the warlike natives of the region. Across the pass you can see a strong contingent of these tribesmen, already occupying the lower heights of a steep hill, which commands the road. Now the Greek advance guard has spotted them too, and it halts. After some hurried delibera- tions you can see a messenger running back. A few minutes later a horseman – it is Xenophon – gallops up to the commander of the advance guard, a seasoned Spartan cap- tain named Chirisophus. Xenophon tells him that he has not brought up a reinforcement of the light-armed troops that had been urgently requested because the rearguard – still under constant attack – could not be weakened. Then he carefully studies the lie of the land. Noticing that the Carduci have neglected to occupy the actual summit of the hill, he puts his plan to his Spartan colleague:

'The best thing to do, Chirisophus, is for us to advance on the summit as fast as we can. If we can occupy it, those who are commanding our road will not be able to main- tain their position. If you like, you stay here with the main body. I will volunteer to go ahead. Or, if you prefer it, you march on the mountain and I will stay here.'

'I will give you the choice,' replies Chirisophus, 'of doing whichever you like.'

It would be an arduous physical ask, Xenophon points out, and he tactfully says that being the younger man he would be the best one to undertake it. Having chosen some 400 skirmishers, armed with targets and light javelins, together with a hundred handpicked pikemen of the advance guard, he marches them off as fast as he can towards the summit.

But when the enemy see what the Greeks are doing, they too begin to head for the highest ground as fast as they can go.

> Then there was a lot of shouting, from the Greek army cheering on its men on the one side and from Tissaphernes' people cheering on their men on the other side. Xenophon rode along the ranks on horseback, urging them on. 'Soldiers,' he said, 'consider that it is for Greece you are fighting now, that you are fighting your way to your children and your wives, and that with a little hard work now, we shall go on the rest of our way unopposed.'
>
> Soteridas, a man from Sicyon, said: 'We are not on a level, Xenophon. You are riding on horseback, while I am wearing myself out with a shield to carry.'

Although he could conceivably have had him arrested and punished later, Xenophon did not take this course. Writing of himself in the third person, he tells us what happened next:

> When Xenophon heard this, he jumped down from his horse, pushed Soteridas out of the ranks, took his shield away from him and went forward on foot as fast as he could, carrying the shield. He happened to be wearing a cavalry breastplate as well, so that it was heavy going for him. He kept on encouraging those in front to keep going and those behind to join up with them, though struggling along behind them himself. The other soldiers, however, struck Soteridas and threw stones at him and cursed him until they forced him to take back his shield and continue marching. Xenophon then remounted and, so long as the going was good, led the way on horseback. When it became impossible to ride, he left his horse behind and hurried ahead on foot. And so they got to the summit before the enemy.

Note that it was the other soldiers who shamed Soteridas into taking back his shield. Although Xenophon, burdened with a heavy cavalry breastplate, eventually fell back behind the ranks as the men rushed up the hill, yet he encouraged the men forward and urged them to keep their battle order. Eventually he remounted and led his soldiers from the front, at first on horse and then again on foot.

Once the Greeks had gained the summit the Carduci turned and fled in all directions. The Persian cavalry under Tissaphernes, who had been distant onlookers of the contest, also turned their bridles and withdrew.

Then Chirisophus' men in the vanguard of the army were able to descend through the mountain pass into a fertile plain beside the Tigris. There they refreshed themselves before facing the fearsome rigours of a winter march amid the snow-covered Armenian highlands. Eventually, in the summer of the following year, the army reached the safety of the Hellespont, the narrow straits dividing Europe from Asia. They owed much to Xenophon who, not long afterwards, became the sole commander of the Ten Thousand.

Anyone reading this story will recognize that in it Xenophon acted as a leader. He led by example. That is a universal principle or theme in the story of leadership. It is especially important where people face hardship or danger: they expect their leaders to run the same risks and shoulder the same burdens as themselves, or at least to show a willingness to do so.

The story of Xenophon's assault on the Carduci illustrates another cardinal principle of leadership. Leaders *encourage* people. They renew spirits, giving others fresh courage to pursue the common course of action. Xenophon's words and deeds infused the Greeks with new confidence and resolution. His brave example inspired them.

A LEADER IN ESTATE MANAGEMENT

After the expedition Xenophon continued to serve as a military commander. He seems to have fallen in love with the profession of arms, though he was also a man of wide-ranging interests. As Athens was in turmoil, Socrates was judicially put to death by enforced suicide about this time – Xenophon chose to live in exile with the Spartans whom he much admired. Not until towards the end of his life did he return home to Athens, and by then he had written some sixteen books and was renowned as one of the most prolific authors in antiquity. Contemporary history, tracts on hunting and horse riding, constitutional studies, texts for educating the young: all flowed from his ready pen. Alexander the Great and Hannibal read and profited from Xenophon's thoughts on leadership. The Romans especially admired him, Julius Caesar and Cicero foremost among them.

For his services to Sparta over many years Xenophon received as a reward a large estate at Scillus, near Mount Olympus, where he lived with his wife and family. It was run as a profit-making business as well as a private estate. Xenophon's book called *Oeconomicus* in Greek (from *oikonomos*, household manager) is the world's first inquiry into the body of laws or branch of knowledge that relates to the management of estates. From the same word we derive our concept of *economy* and the study known today as *economics*. Incidentally, our English word *manage* also derives in part from the management or control of horses. (The first school of management that opened in London in the reign of Queen Elizabeth I was attended by horses and their riders.) Xenophon's book *On Horsemanship* is the oldest extant complete work on the subject, written with all the authority of an expert.

Xenophon did not have much to say about the management of accounts, the origin of our economics. But he was naturally interested in the way that an estate manager – if he was a good leader – could affect the spirits of men at work in the estate fields. He saw a clear parallel here between leadership in the harvest field and leadership on the battlefield: both, he observed with a scientist's eye, had the same positive effect on men. As Xenophon wrote:

Nobody can be a good farmer unless he makes his labourers both eager and obedient; and the captain who leads men against an enemy must contrive to secure the same results by rewarding those who act as brave men should act as punishing the disobedient. And it is no less necessary for the farmer to encourage his labourers often, than for a general to encourage his men. And slaves need the stimulus of good hopes no less, nay, even more than free men, to make them steadfast.

This general leadership ability, as relevant to agriculture as to politics or war, was often absent, he noted, in those who held positions of authority. Xenophon instanced the Greek warships of his day, which were rowed by free men and not by slaves:

On a man-of-war, when the ship is on the high seas and the rowers must toil all day to reach port, some rowing-masters can say and do the right thing to sharpen the men's spirits and make them work with a will. Other boatswains are so unintelligent that it takes them more than twice the time to finish the same voyage. Here they land bathed in sweat, with mutual congratulations, rowing-master and seamen. There they arrive with dry skin; they hate their master and he hates them.

Xenophon's mind ranged back to the generals he had known, who also differed widely from one another in this respect:

> For some make their men unwilling to work and to take risks, disinclined and unwilling to obey, except under compulsion, and actually proud of defying their commander: yes, and they cause them to have no sense of dishonour when something disgraceful occurs. Contrast the genius, the brave and skilful leader: let him take over the command of these same troops, or of others if you like. What effect has he on them? They are ashamed to do a disgraceful act, think it better to obey, and take a pride in obedience, working cheerfully, every man and all together, when it is necessary to work. Just as a love of work may spring up in the mind of a private soldier here and there, so a whole army under the influence of a good leader is inspired by love of work and ambition to distinguish itself under the commander's eye. Let this be the feeling of the rank and file for their commander, then he is the best leader – it is not a matter of being the best with bow and javelin, nor riding the best horse and being foremost in danger, nor being the perfect mounted warrior, but of being able to make his soldiers feel that they must follow him through fire and in any adventure. So, too, in private industries, the man in authority – bailiff or manager – who can make the workers keen, industrious and persevering – he is the man who gives a lift to the business and swells the profits.

ARE LEADERS BORN OR MADE?

For Xenophon, this kind of leadership is quite simply 'the greatest thing in every operation that makes any demand on the labour of men'. If leaders are made in the sense that they can acquire the authority of knowledge, are they born as far as the capacity to inspire is concerned? It is tempting to conclude that this is the case. The ability to give people the intellectual and moral strength to venture or persevere in the presence of danger, fear or difficulty is not the common endowment of all men and women. Xenophon, however, did believe that at least the basic principles of it could be acquired through education, as he had experienced himself with Socrates.

'Mind you, I do not go as far as to say that this can be learnt at sight or at a single hearing,' he wrote in the conclusion of *Oeconomicus*. 'On the contrary, to acquire these powers a man needs education.' Natural potential is most important, he continues. But in some men leadership amounts to a gift, something akin to genius which suggests something more of divine origin than human. This 'power to win willing obedience' may seem ultimately as if it is a gift of the gods, writes Xenophon, but is not capriciously bestowed. The true beneficiaries of it are 'those who devote themselves to seeking wisdom'. There speaks the voice of Socrates!

KEY POINTS: THE WORLD'S FIRST THOUGHTS

This chapter has been devoted to the world's first thoughts – in the person of Xenophon – on strategic leadership. He saw it as a transferable art or skill, and identified its essential principles for the first time. Although nature equipped men and women for leadership – some even having a gift for it – even the best could only develop their natural ability by experience and education. Here is Xenophon's legacy to us:

- Leadership is done from in front. Never ask others to do what you, if challenged, would not be willing to do yourself.
- A leader must be technically and professionally competent in his or her field. You must know your business. This is the main necessary condition for winning respect and trust. It applies to women as well as to men – Xenophon instanced the weaving industry in Athens as one where women were accepted as leaders. *Authority flows to the one who knows.*
- A leader shares fully in the risks, hardships and dangers of the army or workforce. 'Many have often seen him lying on the ground wrapped only in a military cloak amid the sentries and outposts of his soldiers,' wrote the Roman historian Livy of Rome's great enemy, Hannibal. Lead by example.
- A leader inspires others by encouraging them in times of difficulty or challenge, expressing confidence in them and in their ability to surmount the hurdles before them. You can lift people's spirits with a word of encouragement and support.
- A leader reminds people of why they are working and striving – for self, family and comrades certainly, but for that which transcends self.
- A leader has to be firm and just in maintaining necessary order. Without a certain toughness in this regard you will not win the respect of the group as a whole.
- A leader should show humanity, a basic empathy with people. Rejoice with others when any good befalls them, and sympathize when ills overtake them, as they can us all. Give practical help to individual team members in any kind of need where you can do so.
- Above all, a leader is *there* – at the right time and place.

Never underestimate the positive influence that your very presence can exert in a situation.

There is small risk a leader will be regarded with contempt by those he leads if, whatever he may have to ask others to do, he shows himself best able to inform.

Xenophon

2

THE MILITARY ROOTS OF
STRATEGIC LEADERSHIP

'Dux erat ille ducum.'
'He was the leader of leaders', Ovid, Heroides

'Do you know when managers began to talk about strategy?' management consultant Peter Drucker asked during the course of a seminar we were leading together.

'I imagine it was sometime . . . no, I really don't know,' I replied. 'When was it?'

'In 1964 I submitted a book to my American publisher,' he said, 'which I had called *Management Strategy*. They insisted that I should change the title, as "strategy" was a military term and business executive readers would either not understand it or perceive it as irrelevant. So it appeared as *Management for Results*.'

'Where did the idea come from to bring in the concept of strategy in the first place?' I asked.

'I believe it stemmed from Robert McNamara in the Kennedy era,' Drucker replied. 'McNamara moved between heading up the Pentagon as Secretary of Defense to being President of the Ford Motor Company.'

In fact one or two books did appear about that time that

used the word *strategy* in the business context, notably Alfred D. Chandler's *Strategy and Structure: Chapters in the History of American Industrial Enterprise* (1962) and Igor Ansoff's *Corporate Strategy* (1965). But, as far as I know, I was the first to introduce the concept of *strategic leadership* in the 1980s and it is now in wide use.

Originally, as we have seen, strategy (*strategia* in Greek) meant strategic leadership – the art of being a commander-in-chief. Therefore, inadvertently and through no fault of their own, these early business gurus were making the same errors as Dionysodorus. They were mistaking a part for the whole and also teaching it in an academic and wooden manner.

'*Ad Fontes*' – 'Back to the Foundations' – was the personal motto of the Renaissance scholar Thomas Linacre, an eminent doctor and a founder member of the Royal College of Physicians. In order to understand the concept of strategic leadership we must explore its roots in the tangled undergrowth of military history, which stretches back 2,500 years to the Age of Xenophon. Only by this process can we root out some of the misconceptions that, like gigantic weeds, tend to dominate the modern idea of a strategic leader.

THE OVER-EMPHASIS OF STRATEGY

Just as in the days of Xenophon battlefield tactics were only one aspect of *strategia*, not the whole. So, in later times, campaign strategy was only one aspect of being a commander-in-chief, not the whole. The misconception that campaign strategy is the *dominant* work of a general is comparatively recent in origin. It has led to an over-emphasis on the importance of strategic thinking.

Veni, vidi, vici. As the proverbial schoolboy knows, 'I

came, I saw, I conquered' is Julius Caesar's laconic summary of his campaign in Gaul. Although not the first general to write a memoir of his campaigns – Xenophon has that to his credit – Caesar was certainly not the last. Like his successors, however, he tells us virtually nothing about strategy or about himself as a strategic thinker.

The tendency to reduce strategic leadership or generalship in the military field to *strategy* in the narrow sense really dates from the twentieth century, paradoxically at a time when the evolution of telecommunications was eroding more and more of a general's freedom of action.

Given the realities of the situation, strategy in the military field is usually simple. It is also commonly the product of many minds. When generals in modern times – Montgomery is a good example – write their memoirs, especially if they tend to be egotistical, they exaggerate their own role in devising strategy and correspondingly denigrate the contribution from others, be it their superiors, colleagues or predecessors.

THE ART OF GENERALSHIP

If we look at it historically, strategy – strategic thinking and planning – is never more than half of what a commander-in-chief, the prototypical strategic leader, should be doing. War is like wrestling or playing chess in that there are only a finite number of possibilities. These strategic options are easily available to a general of average or above-average intelligence who knows his business and has served his apprenticeship under other commanders good or bad.

WELLINGTON LEARNS HIS LESSONS

The British Army in the later eighteenth century was unprofessional, inadequately trained and under-resourced. Any coherent system of command and control and of administration, and any tradition of commitment and loyalty were lacking. Wellington had acquired first-hand experience of the situation during the Duke of York's disastrous campaign in the Netherlands in 1794–95. 'I learned more by seeing our own faults, and the defects of our system in the campaign in Holland than anywhere else,' he claimed. He later observed that, 'I learned what one ought not to do, and that is always something.' During the next twenty years, first in India, then in the Peninsula, he set about creating an army with a sense of confidence and achievement that could and would defeat Napoleon.

Even the strategic ideas are simple. Since the study of Napoleon's campaigns, one of the chief ones has been concentration of force. The underlying principle here is the concentration of superior force at the decisive time and place, the main point of effort, while economizing elsewhere. For it is impossible to be strong everywhere and, if decisive strength is to be concentrated at the critical time and place, there must be no wasteful expenditure of effort and resources that cannot significantly affect the issue.

Surprise is another example of a basic strategic idea. The Greek called on artifice or tricks in war, for surprising, deceiving and outwitting an enemy and a *strategema*, (derived from *strategia*), to be a general. From it we derive our word stratagem. Surprise always acts as a bonus in war, and it can have a devastating effect on an enemy not least for psychological reasons: its elements are secrecy, timely intelligence, deception, concealment, audacity and speed.

Timing is the key factor. It may be difficult to achieve at strategic level, but even so, it may still be achieved at operational and team levels. Surprise of itself doesn't deliver success but it is often a principal factor in achieving it.

Strategy will always be a simple matter, with some surprise thrown in for good measure. But, as Clausewitz said, 'In war what counts is doing simple things, but in war it is very difficult to do simple things.' It is overcoming these areas of difficulty – quite apart from strategy – that constitutes the other core elements in the art of the commander-in-chief. 'Strategy' is only one exam paper that a general has to answer in the field; here are three others of equal importance.

MORALE

How do you build and sustain the spirit of the army as a whole? How can you restore confidence if it has suffered reverses? How can you generate the will to win?

General Eisenhower had to take a crash course in strategic leadership in order to pass this exam paper. He had no direct experience of war when he was appointed as commander-in-chief of the US Army, which landed in North Africa in 1943. Rommel's experienced German Panzer troops inflicted a severe defeat on the Americans at Kasserine Pass. In his headquarters in Gibraltar, Eisenhower was despondent. But he learned there the most important lesson of all. Optimism spreads down from the Supreme Commander but pessimism spreads down even faster. He saw that it was critical in a leadership role to exude optimism and to radiate a sense of self-confidence. 'I firmly determined,' he said later, 'that my mannerisms and speech would always reflect cheerful certainty. Without optimism in command, victory is scarcely attainable.'

Morale is the mental and emotional attitude of a person or a group to the function or task expected of them. It comes from the French *moral*, re-spelt to indicate stress of pronunciation (like the word *locale*). Cicero invented the word *moral* in Latin as a translation of the Greek *ethikos*, pertaining to a person's character.

Confidence, hope, zeal, willingness: all these are expressions of morale. Rather like shares on the stock exchange, they fluctuate up and down. Sometimes these movements are so slight that you may hardly notice them. At other times, however, the fall is much more noticeable. It is an essential function of a strategic leader – in partnership with operational and team leaders – to build and maintain a high level of morale.

The reason for such a high strategic priority is that morale is a fuel gauge indicating the sense of common purpose with respect to a group – close to what the French call *esprit de corps*, the common spirit existing in members of a group and inspiring enthusiasm, devotion and a strong regard for its honour. That sense of common purpose is the aligned and focused energy of the group or organization. If that energy is diminished in any way, an organization's effectiveness is thereby depleted as well.

The military has long understood that fact, and also the dynamic relationship between leadership and morale. Since about 1830 the word morale has been used in English to cover the moral condition, conduct or behaviour of a body of soldiers when it comes to such matters as confidence, willingness to go forward and discipline in adversity. It has long been recognized as a battle-winning (or -losing) factor, and 'Maintenance of Morale' comes second in the list of Principles of War only to 'Selection and Maintenance of the Aim'.

Because success in military operations depends as much

on the morale factor as upon the scale of personnel involved or the quantity and quality of material deployed, high morale is probably the single most important factor across the spectrum of conflict, ranging from full-scale war to peace-keeping activities. But the principle applies to all organizations.

The common issue of morale is the basic mental and emotional attitude to the common task. The confidence in question is the confidence of victory, success or achievement. That is why failures or reverses tend to lower morale. It follows that morale can only be boosted by successes of the prospect of ultimate success. To provide better food, better offices or better pay cannot have more than a momentary effect on morale. For money or material factors cannot buy what is essentially a matter of the spirit.

SUSTAINABILITY

Administration is the activity of sustaining an army during every stage of a campaign. Following French military usage, there is a distinction between *personnel* – the people involved – and *materiel* – the sum of equipment, weapons and expendable commodities. Administration encompasses all these aspects.

Logistics (from the Greek *logistike*, the art of calculating) is the science of the procurement, maintenance and trans-portation of military materiel, facilities and personnel. In wider use it now refers to the detailed organization and implementation of a plan or operation. No plan can succeed without logistic support commensurate to the aim of the campaign or operation. It follows, therefore, that a strategic leader must have a degree of control over the logistical side of the plan that matches his or her level of accountability.

Scarce resources should be controlled at the strategic level, and the logistic organization must be flexible enough to respond to changes of plan in the most economic way.

Great captains of war have always been strong on administration, not least because it directly affects battle effectiveness – even the bravest need ammunition – and because poor administration adversely affects morale. As armies grew in size and complexity, operating over great distances from home base, so administration called for a higher order of the art of calculating. 'You need to know mathematics,' Napoleon commented to one of his entourage, General Gourgaud, who accompanied him into exile on St. Helena and subsequently wrote Napoleon's memoirs. 'That is useful in a thousand circumstances to correct ideas. Perhaps I owe my success to my mathematical ideas; a general must never make a picture for himself. That is the worst thing of all.'

Napoleon's tendency to calculate – to determine things by mathematical processes – applied to his military operations as well. 'I am used to thinking three or four months in advance about what I must do, and I calculate on the worst,' he explained to his brother Joseph. 'In war nothing is achieved except by calculations. Everything that is not soundly planned in its details yields no results.' Napoleon was not a man to leave things to chance.

Apart from inducing an almost scientific sense of objectivity and a natural ability to calculate the odds, the mathematics that Napoleon had acquired as a young artillery officer served him well as an administrator. His brain could work like a computer, which helped. 'A very curious thing about me is my memory,' he told Gaspard Gourgaud. 'As a young man I knew the logarithms of more than thirty to forty numbers. I knew, in France, not only the names of the officers of all regiments, but the places where the regiments were recruited and gained distinction.'

This prodigious memory and his infinite capacity for mastering detail – much of it administrative – set Napoleon apart from most men. He constantly fretted in letters to his generals about the need for them to pay strict attention to their muster rolls:

> The good condition of my armies comes from the fact that I devote an hour or two every day to them, and when I am sent the returns of my troops and my ships each month, which fills twenty large volumes, I set every other occupation aside to read them in detail in order to discern the difference that exists from one month to another. I take greater pleasure in this reading than a young lady would get from reading a novel.

Napoleon kept his critical eye on every detail of logistics. 'The direction of military affairs [i.e. strategy] is only half the work of a general,' he insisted. One large segment of the half centred upon morale, the maintenance of the *esprit de corps* of the army and its famous *élan* – the energy, ardour and dash arising from enthusiasm. But Napoleon may well have regarded the shielding of the 'sacred flame' as he called it, as part of the direction of military affairs, and needless to say he was a master of this aspect of personal leadership. His very presence could transform the mood of the army. Wellington once remarked: 'I used to say of him [Napoleon] that his presence on the field made the difference of forty thousand men.'

No, the other half was a detailed knowledge of the workings of the military machine. It is true that Napoleon delegated the day-to-day running of the machine to his various chiefs-of-staff. The greatest of them was Marshal Berthier, whose absence in the Waterloo campaign undoubtedly contributed to Napoleon's ultimate defeat. The

Emperor's workload was made tolerable by his absorbing interest in the details of military activity, including everything to do with logistics. When asked one day how, after so many years, he could recall the statistics of his units and the names of their commanders, Napoleon replied: 'Madam, this is a lover's recollection of his former mistresses.'

Organization and administration go hand-in-hand. The prime purpose of the former is to establish a framework of responsibilities through and by means of which the concern may do its job. The prime purpose of the latter is to make the organization work; this includes, as one of its principal purposes, the removal of every avoidable obstacle from the way of the people who are actually doing the job. These obstacles may be material, human or organizational: but they all are fundamentally the concern of administration.

CASE STUDY: FIELD MARSHAL MONTGOMERY

On 13 August 1942 Montgomery arrived to take command of the Eighth Army, two months before the Battle of Alamein. 'The atmosphere was dismal and dreary', he wrote in his diary. That evening he addressed the entire staff of Army Headquarters, between fifty and sixty officers. As he was their fourth Army Commander within a year, he faced a sceptical audience. The seasoned commanders and staff officers plainly doubted that this new general from Britain was the man to reverse their recent defeats and failures. Montgomery knew that he had to win their minds and hearts that evening if the morale of that broken army was to be restored to full pitch.

He stood on the steps of his predecessor's caravan and bade the gathering sit on the sand. He spoke without notes, looking straight at his audience. Here is what he said:

I want first of all to introduce myself to you. You do not know me. I do not know you. But we have got to work together; therefore we must understand each other and we must have confidence in one another. I have only been here a few hours. But from what I have seen and heard since I arrived I am prepared to say, here and now, that I have confidence in you. We will then work together as a team; and together we will gain the confidence of this great army and go forward to final victory in Africa.

I believe that one of the first duties of a commander is to create what I call 'atmosphere'; and in that atmosphere, his staff, subordinate commanders and troops will live and work and fight.

I do not like the general atmosphere I find here. It is an atmosphere of doubt, of looking back to select the next place to which to withdraw, of loss of confidence in our ability to defeat Rommel, of desperate defence measures by reserves in preparing positions in Cairo and the Delta. All that must cease. Let us have a new atmosphere ... We will stand and fight here. If we can't stay here alive, then let us stay here dead.

I want to impress on everyone that the bad times are over. Fresh divisions from the UK are now arriving in Egypt, together with ample reinforcements for our present divisions. We have 300 to 400 new Sherman tanks coming and these are actually being unloaded at Suez now. Our mandate from the Prime Minister is to destroy the Axis forces in North Africa; I have seen it written on half a sheet of notepaper. And it will be done. If anyone here thinks it can't be done, let him to at once; I don't want any doubters in this party. It can be done, and it will be done; beyond any possibility of doubt ...

What I have done is to get over to you the atmosphere in which we will now work and fight; you must see that that atmosphere permeates right down through the Eighth

Army to the most junior private soldier. All the soldiers must know what is wanted; when they see it coming to pass, there will be a surge of confidence throughout the army.

I ask you to give me your confidence and to have faith that what I have said will come to pass.

There is much work to be done. The orders I have given about no further withdrawal will mean a complete change in our dispositions; also that we must begin to prepare for our great offensive . . .

'The great point to remember,' Montgomery concluded at that famous initial briefing, 'is that we are going to finish with this chap Rommel once and for all. It will be quite easy. There is no doubt about that. He is definitely a nuisance. Therefore we will hit him a crack and finish with him.'

As Montgomery stepped down the officers rose and stood to attention. 'One could have heard a pin drop if such a thing were possible in the sand of the desert,' recollected Montgomery. 'But it certainly had a profound effect, and a spirit of hope, anyway of clarity, was born that evening.' His Chief-of-Staff, General de Guingand, agreed: 'It was one of his greatest efforts,' he wrote. 'The effect of the address was electric – it was terrific! And we all went to bed that night with new hope in our hearts, and a great confidence in the future of our Army. I wish someone had taken it down in shorthand, for it would have become a classic of its kind.' Fortunately, it *was* taken down in shorthand and filed away for many years before appearing in print for the first time in 1981.

COOPERATION

Napoleon was beaten at Waterloo not by Wellington alone but by the combination of the British and Prussian armies. Most successful military operations are joint enterprises, involving in these days cooperation between the three services – army, navy and airforce – the civil authorities, and between allies. Goodwill, a common aim and a clear division of responsibilities, based upon an understanding of the capabilities and limitations of the others involved, are necessary conditions for such cooperation. A strategic leader's role includes forging alliances and making them work well.

Within alliances and conditions, where nations may not have identical interests but share a specific common aim, that key strategic responsibility may call for considerable political skills if the alliance is to be kept healthy. The Duke of Marlborough's dealings with Britain's Dutch ally in the early eighteenth-century wars against France, is a copy-book example of how it should be done. But some generals fail this particular exam paper in strategic leadership in a spectacular way. Montgomery, for example, was unable to work harmoniously with his US counterparts nor under Eisenhower as Allied Supreme Commander. In his own phrase, he had reached his ceiling. By contrast, Generals Alexander and Slim were both exceptionally good at building strong relations with their allies.

Not that it was always easy. After his lecture to managers on leadership in 1948, Slim was asked if there were any parallels with negotiations with trade unions in the forces, a pressing topic for a British industry divided between the 'us' and 'them' of unionized labour and management. Slim drew an analogy with dealing with allies:

I speak from very little experience of trade unions but with a great deal of experience of allies. Russians, Chinese, French, Americans, Iraqis, Syrians, the Lord knows what! They were all at times absolutely exasperating. Try conducting negotiations with a Chinese general or a Russian, and see how you get on! But what I always found was that I could get the thing in perspective by remembering that I was an 'ally' myself.

'Get the trade union leaders to see that you are both on the same side, like allies in a common cause,' he concluded.

POLITICS

As a general principle the consequence of moving to the strategic level of leadership responsibility is that you move either suddenly or imperceptibly into the domain of politics. This principle in turn is part of an even wider one, namely that it is increasing complexity that distinguishes one level of leadership from another.

It follows that a mind honed to deal with military complexity by reducing it to simple essentials may not be equally equipped to handle political complexity. As we have just seen, the ability to cooperate effectively with allies implies an understanding of their different political agendas and some tact if not diplomatic skill. Similar political awareness, understanding and skill is called for in relation to what generals in democratic countries tend to refer to as their 'political masters'. Politicians are not always universally esteemed but in a democracy they are on top and – subject to certain safeguards – military forces owe their loyalty to their elected governments. Moreover, the principle articulated by Carl von Clausewitz, the Prussian military historian and author of *Vom Kriege* (*On War*) – but certainly not invented by him – that war is never an end in itself but always a means to a political end, ordains that a commander-in-chief must work in harmony with the political leader-in-chief. For the latter, in our Clausewitzian world, is the ultimate arbiter or strategy.

Like all human relations, the basis for a successful partnership between a military commander-in-chief and a political strategic leader-in-chief is mutual trust and respect. This in turn implies good communication. For the better the communicator, the more the trust; the more trust, the more that can be communicated. As the proverb says: 'The wing carries the bird, but the bird carries the wings.'

In the Second World War some British generals like Wavell and Auchinleck, who were 'stiff upper lipped' in the mould of Wellington, lost their jobs because Churchill found them too inarticulate. They were not men who would stoop to trying to sell themselves. Both had strong professional reputations. Wavell could certainly communicate well in other situations – he lectured on leadership at St. Andrew's University and wrote a short book 'On Generalship'. But he failed one of the examination papers of modern military strategic leadership: he seemed tongue-tied in Churchill's presence and could not throw that first line across the river that would eventually lead to the building of a bridge of trust.

Other generals could do it. Eisenhower was gifted in this respect. As Allied Supreme Commander he forged an excellent working relationship with Churchill based on mutual confidence in each other's qualities as leaders in their respective fields:

When Sir Winston Churchill died, the spontaneous outpouring of admiration and affection from all over the world was a tribute to a great and noble man. But it was more than that; it was also a shining testimonial to the qualities of leadership. This world has always set a high value on leadership, and in the person of Sir Winston people everywhere found a superb combination of those characteristics which lift and inspire the human spirit.

I have long suspected that men who possess the capacity for leadership are always among us – waiting in the wings – but it sometimes takes a great crisis to bring them to prominence. The turbulent period in which I have lived has produced its share of outstanding leaders, and it has been my good fortune to know a number of them.

These were the opening words of Eisenhower's article on 'What is Leadership?' (*The Reader's Digest*, July 1965). It gives us some glimpses of Eisenhower's extraordinary ability to establish partnerships with supervisors of very different personalities, such as the US Chief-of-Staff General Marshall, and Churchill:

It would be hard to imagine two men more unlike, in external traits, than General Marshall and Winston Churchill. Marshall was remote in manner, often abrupt. I knew no man who could call him an intimate friend. Churchill was convivial, outgoing, full of humour. The give-and-take of conferences delighted him; he liked people, and people instantly liked him. Yet both men had the same inner qualities of heart and mind that made them great leaders.

Mutual liking is not enough, it has to be backed by mutual respect. Here a political leader-in-chief has to demonstrate a grasp of the broad strategic issues, not least because the one or two big strategic decisions in a war have to be taken by the politician acting on professional advice, not by the commander-in-chief alone. General MacArthur, the commander-in-chief in the Korean War, lost his job for appearing to challenge President Truman's prerogative to decide on such a major strategic issue as the employment of tactical nuclear weapons against the Chinese.

President Truman had served as a front-line artillery officer in the First World War, but his predecessor Franklin D. Roosevelt had no military experience; indeed, crippled by polio as a young man, Roosevelt was bound to a wheelchair. Yet Eisenhower was impressed by his strategic grasp and sheer application:

> I never knew President Roosevelt as well as I did some of the other world leaders, but in the few conferences I had with him I was impressed, not only by his inspirational qualities, but by his amazing grasp of the whole complex war effort. He could discuss strategy on equal terms with his generals and admirals. His knowledge of the geography of the war theatres was so encyclopaedic that the most obscure places in far-away countries were always accurately sited on his mental map. President Roosevelt possessed personality, but as his nation's leader, in a global conflict, he also did his homework – thoroughly.

All strategic leaders have to find their way through complex political situations. Some – the strategic leaders in charge of large government departments, for example, or chief executives in local government – will have direct deals with elected political leaders. They will need Eisenhower's ability to establish common ground and build a professional but warm partnership. Equally, however, political leaders must learn to be *leaders* – strategic leaders of the calibre of Churchill and Roosevelt who command respect by their strategic grasp of the business in question. Who is to train senior politicians throughout the world to be such effective strategic leaders? Solve that problem and the world takes a quantum step forwards.

ON GENERALSHIP

It is interesting to see the role of a *strategos* – the leader of a whole army – through the eyes of a chief-of-staff. By definition a chief-of-staff works closely with a commander-in-chief and their roles are complementary, and so it is a professional equivalent to marriage. Indeed, a chief-of-staff can fulfil some of the functions of a wife in restoring a degree of harmony when her difficult spouse is apparently intent on disrupting them. Montgomery was fortunate to have as his chief-of-staff a man with a talent for diplomacy.

In 1946 Sir Francis de Guingand, a knight and a major-general at the age of forty-four, retired from the army. He had been Field Marshal Montgomery's chief-of-staff from the Battle of El Alamein until the end of the war in Europe, and Montgomery, on becoming Chief of the General Staff, failed to appoint him as his vice, contrary to his previously stated intentions.

In his autobiography *From Brass Hat to Bowler Hat* (Hamish Hamilton, 1979) de Guingand tells of the events leading to his resignation and of the way in which he employed the talents that had made him an outstanding chief-of-staff to carve out a second career as an industrialist in South Africa. Interesting as these reminiscences are, the book is more important for the light that the author, who was closely involved with all three, throws on the characters and relationships of Auchinleck, Montgomery and Eisenhower.

Perhaps the greatest contribution de Guingand made to the Allied victory was in preventing an outright breach between Montgomery and Eisenhower while remaining loyal to the one and retaining the friendship of the other. Of Auchinleck he writes:

Montgomery detested him ... This was a shame, for Auchinleck's contribution to ultimate British victory in the Western Desert is indisputable ... When Rommel subsequently counter-attacked ... it was Auchinleck's personal assumption of command that restored the situation and paved the way for the successful defence of Alam Halfa.

De Guingand remained on close terms with Eisenhower and Montgomery until the end of their lives and indeed helped to smooth ruffled feathers in what might be termed the 'Battle of the Memoirs'. As he writes: 'Once more as in the war, I found myself trying to keep the peace between Eisenhower and Montgomery, not always an easy task. They were in almost every respect opposites; yet each in his own way a genius.'

Montgomery, he adds, 'never possessed Eisenhower's breadth of vision, transparent humility or nobility: but at the deadly business of war, the task of making a largely amateur army first equal, then superior to, a highly disciplined, indoctrinated enemy he had no rival.'

In his earlier book *Operation Victory* (1947) de Guingand offered 'Six points for successful generalship' that apply to any strategic leader, not merely military ones. A general must:

- Know his 'stuff' thoroughly
- Be known and recognized by the troops

- Ensure that the troops are given tasks that are within their powers. Success means mutual confidence – failure the reverse
- See that his subordinate commanders are disturbed as little as possible in carrying out their tasks
- Command by personal contact
- Be human and study the human factor

De Guingand continues: 'Many times during the war I have tried to analyse the ingredients of the "big man". The following are the points that I consider important:'

- He should be able to sit back and avoid getting immersed in detail
- He must be a good 'picker' of men
- He should trust those under him, and let them get on with their job without interference
- He must have the power of clear decision
- He should inspire confidence
- He should not be pompous

A business leader who read this list commented to me: 'Any good chairman or chief executive should be able to identify with those qualities. More importantly, perhaps, his or her board colleagues should be able to recognize them when appointments are being made.'

De Guingand's profile tells us much about what a chief-of-staff *expects* from a commander-in-chief. It is the work of a general. In order to make it possible the staff, under direction of its chief, have to take as much as possible of the load of detailed planning, logistics and administration off the general's shoulders, leaving him free to think, to lead and to oversee the whole operation – including key relations with allies and political leaders. Behind every great commander-in-chief lies a great chief-of-staff. What would Napoleon have been without Marshal Berthier? Have a look at the Battle of Waterloo and there is your answer!

THE ROLE OF A STRATEGIC LEADER

'The Leaders of Industry,' wrote Thomas Carlyle in 1843, 'are virtually Captains of the World.' Although Xenophon had first explored the parallels between war and business it was not until the rise of industrial giants – notably the railways – in the nineteenth century that business leaders could be mentioned in the same breath as the great captains – Wellington and Napoleon, Grant and Lee. It was perhaps symbolic that General Robert E. Lee became president of the first business school in the US. Were not men like Andrew Carnegie or John D. Rockefeller, heads of organizations that dwarfed armies in size and resources, the new commanders-in-chief of the post-Industrial Revolution?

To those industrial organizations of all shapes and sizes we must add others in many fields – such as health, education, science, sport, the arts, politics and religion. Given that the roots of strategic leadership go down so deeply into the military tradition, is it really possible to disentangle them, as it were, from their bloodstained soil and come up with a generic set of functions?

That is a question I shall leave hanging tantalizingly in the air. For the way to answer it is, in my opinion, not to try to work directly from military to civilian practice, modifying or adapting one to the other. It is better to be radical and explore the deeper common root which feeds all particular manifestations or field-specific forms – leadership.

KEY POINTS: THE MILITARY ROOTS OF STRATEGIC LEADERSHIP

- Strategy as a word is a fairly recent borrowing from the military vocabulary. It reflects its more modern military usage – strategy as opposed to tactics.
- In fact this modern idea of strategy is far too narrow. Strategy or *strategia*, properly understood, is the leadership of a large body of people, such as a *stratos* – an army spread out. As armies were the largest work-related organizations for some 3,000 years before the rise of big business in the nineteenth century, it is not surprising that the concept of strategic leadership developed into its first full-blown form in the role of a commander-in-chief.
- The contemporary tendency to equate strategic leadership with formulating strategy reflects a basic misunderstanding of the concept. If you look closely at effective military leaders, strategy in the narrow sense occupies only a small amount of their time.
- A large amount of any general's daily work is administration – ensuring the sustainability of an army. Much of it, given the military staff system that has evolved over centuries, can be delegated. But delegation is not the same as abdication. Sustainability is so important that a commander-in-chief must always have oversight of it.
- The parallels between leadership in different fields soon become apparent to those who study them. The higher the level of leadership responsibility, the closer they seem to become.
- This suggests that leadership – be it teams or organizations – is like a substance that can be moulded into different forms without losing its intrinsic nature. An exploration of that 'substance', with examples from different fields to

make it concrete, should lead us to a more generic role of strategic leadership than this review of generalship can afford us. It's worth a try!

KENT *You have a look upon your face that I would fain call master.*
LEAR *What is that?*
KENT *Authority.*

William Shakespeare, *King Lear*, Act I, scene iv

3

WHAT IS LEADERSHIP?

'Not the cry but the flight of the wild duck leads
the flock to fly and to follow.'

Chinese proverb

What is leadership? I first asked myself this question when I
was just eighteen and coming to the end of my schooldays
at St. Paul's School in London. I had chosen to give a lecture
on the subject 'Leadership in History' to the school historical
society, which I had founded. Someone present wrote this
brief summary of my talk for the school magazine:

> Leadership, he said, could be defined as the activity of
> influencing people to pursue a certain course; there must
> also be some power of mind behind the leader. Leadership
> is not merely the authority of the commander, but con-
> tains by necessity some strange strength of personality
> which attracts the ordinary man. It is only when the times
> are favourable that a man of destiny can come into his
> own. Although leadership may change in this aspect from
> age to age, the qualities of a leader are the same.

Many years later, having devoted much of my professional
life to leadership and leadership development, I find that this

summary is not far off the mark in reflecting what I think today. Sometimes first thoughts are best.

The year was 1952, seven years after the end of the Second World War. A week later Field Marshal Montgomery came to lecture to the sixth form. He had been a pupil at St. Paul's School and he had also used our red-brick school building in Hammersmith to house his planning staff before Operation Overlord in 1944. We gathered to hear him in the lecture room where he and Eisenhower had once briefed King George VI and Winston Churchill on the plans for D-Day.

At precisely 11am Monty, as we all called him, strode on to the platform, wearing battle-dress with ten rows of coloured medal ribbons. He had a narrow, foxy face, sharp, intelligent and tenacious, with very bright and clear blue eyes and a small, slight, spare body. He had a look on his face of extreme attention and sagacity, like a very alert terrier. This was the completely self-confident man who had taken over command of a somewhat demoralized Eighth Army, restored its fighting spirit and led it to the first British victory of the Second World War.

Alone on the platform with a large map as a visual aid, Monty spoke to us about the Alamein campaign for an hour without notes, as if he had been briefing his divisional commanders. Clarity and confidence hallmarked every sentence. As Brigadier Essame wrote about him in Ronald Lewin's *Montgomery as a Military Commander* (1971):

> He could describe a complex situation with amazing lucidity and sum up a long exercise without the use of a single note. He looked straight into the eyes of the audience when he spoke. He had a remarkable flair for picking out the essence of a problem, and for indicating its solution with startling clarity. It was almost impossible

to misunderstand his meaning, however unpalatable it might be.

Such was the impression he made on me. Over lunch in the High Master's room I asked Monty his secret of leadership. How did he lead such a large army to victory? Of his reply I can remember now only one sentence: 'I made my soldiers partners with me in the battle.' When my first book *Training for Leadership* appeared in 1968, Monty took the trouble to write to me in his own clear hand:

> Leadership is an immense subject. In 1961 I published a book entitled *The Path to Leadership* (Collins), in which I tried to show the way towards it. And in 1945 I gave a lecture at St Andrew's University in Scotland on 'Military Leadership'.
>
> Nowhere is it more important to teach it than at Sandhurst and in our universities; in fact to youth, since it falls on dead ground with the older generation.

By 1952 there were political moves afoot to abolish military conscription, which Churchill had insisted should be called National Service. In the context of the Cold War, Montgomery insisted upon its retention, and so I owe it in part to him that I served as a soldier for a compulsory two years after leaving school. Not that I minded – I was looking forward to the adventure.

In the army I encountered two theories of leadership, as they might be called. One – the Qualities or Traits Approach – I had largely been working with already. The other – the Functional Approach, as I named it – was implicit in the selection system for officers but not overt. Long after my military service I came to see that there were in fact *three* distinct approaches to understanding leadership – Qualities,

Situational and Functional – and it is that fuller conceptual sketch map that I follow below.

THE QUALITIES APPROACH

'The qualities of a leader are the same,' I had said at St. Paul's School. When I eventually got to Eaton Hall Officer Training Unit in 1953 we were given a student précis that defined leadership as 'the art of influencing a body of people to follow a certain course of action; the art of controlling them, directing them and getting the best out of them.' Seventeen qualities were then listed, each with a brief note of explanation:

- Ability to make decisions
- Energy
- Assurance (Confidence)
- Determination
- Example
- Resolute courage
- Calmness in crisis
- Sense of justice
- Human element
- Initiative
- Pride in command
- Loyalty
- Sense of duty
- Humour
- Ability to accept responsibility
- Physical fitness
- Enthusiasm

'These qualities make a good leader but never imagine you have learnt all about leadership,' concluded the précis. 'You will always have something more to learn, so be prepared to profit by experience. Experience helps a great deal. Take every opportunity of gaining experience in leadership. Being an officer and a leader is a big job, a fine job and a thoroughly worthwhile job. See that you become a leader in the early and best sense of the word.' That was all that we were taught directly about leadership.

Meanwhile the Qualities Approach – an instance of which is on page 55 – was falling out of favour in the US. Some psychologists had already pointed out the discrepancies between the various lists of leadership qualities derived from what purported to be objective or empirical studies of actual leaders. The assumption that there is a set of leadership qualities that characterized all leaders in all fields at all times was questioned and then abandoned. In its place came the view that leadership was situationally determined. There were no universal qualities: it all depended upon what attributes were required in a specific situation. In the box below you will find some examples of these early research findings, but feel free to skip them if your interests are not academic.

Research into leadership qualities

1. Professor Bird of the University of Minnesota looked at approximately twenty studies 'bearing some resemblance to controlled investigations' that contained seventy-nine traits. 'Surprisingly little overlapping is found from study to study. Actually 51 or 65 per cent are mentioned once, 16 or 20 per cent are common to two lists, 4 or 5 per cent are found in three, and another 5 per cent in four lists. Two traits are common to five lists, and one trait, namely, initiative, to six, and another one, high intelligence, to ten lists.

   C. Bird, *Social Psychology*, pp. 378–9 (D. Appleton-Century, New York and London, 1940)

2. The writers of one article have 17,000 words used to describe qualities of personality.

   G. W. Allport and H. A. Odbert, 'Trait-names: A Psycholexical Study', *Psychological Monographs*, no. 211 (1936)

3. R. M. Stogdill, who studied the evidence for twenty-nine qualities appearing in 124 studies, concluded that although

intelligence, scholarliness, dependability, social participation and socio-economic status were found to bear some relation to leadership, the evidence suggests that leadership is a relationship that exists between persons in a social situation, and that persons who are leaders in one situation may not necessarily be leaders in other situations.

R. M. Stogdill, 'Personal Factors Associated with Leadership: A Survey of the Literature', *Journal of Psychology*, vol. 25, pp. 35–71 (1948)

4. Another study by W. O. Jenkins, published a year earlier in 1947, supports this conclusion. After reviewing seventy-four studies on military leadership the author wrote:

> Leadership is specific to the particular situation under investigation. Who becomes the leader of a particular group engaging in a particular activity and what the leadership characteristics are in the given case are a function of the specific situation ... [there are] wide variations in the characteristics of individuals who become leaders in similar situations and even great divergence in leadership behaviour in different situations ... The only common factor appeared to be that leaders in a particular field need and tend to possess superior general or technical competence or knowledge in that area. General intelligence does not seem to be the answer ...

W. O. Jenkins, 'A Review of Leadership Studies with Particular Reference to Military Problems', *Psychological Bulletin*, vol. 44, pp. 54–79 (1947)

The intellectual and emotional rejection of the Qualities Approach reflected some of the cultural values in US society in the post-Second World War period. Many of those in the burgeoning field of the social or behavioural sciences had emigrated from a Europe where the German and Italian words for leader were *Führer* and *Duce*. It was an anti-leadership culture, in so far as leadership was seen to be vested in an individual by virtue of possessing the 'qualities of leadership'. The group replaced the leader as the centre of attention.

William H. Whyte caught this mood perfectly in *The Organization Man* (1955). 'Anti-authoritarianism is becoming anti-leadership,' he wrote. 'In group doctrine the strong personality is viewed with overwhelming suspicion. The cooperative are those who take a stance directly over the keel; the man with ideas – in translation, prejudices – leans to one side or, worse yet, heads for the rudder.'

The trouble with 'group leadership' was that, while it may have been effective in the artificial situations for research and training known in America as 'group laboratories' it could not be and was not effective in the real world of work. One of the first to see this truth was Douglas McGregor, a former professor of psychology at the Massachusetts Institute of Technology and author of the widely influential book *The Human Side of Enterprise* (1960). In 1948 McGregor was appointed head of Antioch University and there he learnt that being a college president meant exercising personal leadership. Here are his conclusions:

> The first is a conviction that has been derived from my personal struggle with the role of college president. Before coming to Antioch I had observed and worked with top executives as an adviser in a number of organizations. I thought I knew how they felt about their responsibilities and what led them to behave as they did. I even thought that I could create a role for myself that would enable me to avoid some of the difficulties they encountered. I was wrong! It took the direct experience of becoming a line

executive, and meeting personally the problems involved, to teach me what no amount of observation of other people could have taught.

I believed, for example, that a leader could operate successfully as a kind of adviser to his organization. I thought I could avoid being a 'boss'. Unconsciously, I suspect, I hoped to duck the unpleasant necessity of making difficult decisions, of taking the responsibility for one course of action among many uncertain alternatives, of making mistakes and taking the consequences. I thought that maybe I could operate so that everyone would like me – that 'good human relations' would eliminate all discord and disagreement.

I could not have been more wrong. It took a couple of years, but I finally began to realize that a leader cannot avoid the exercise of authority any more than he can avoid responsibility for what happens to his organization. In fact, it is a major function of the top executive to take on his own shoulders the responsibility for resolving the uncertainties that are always involved in important decisions. Moreover, since no important decision ever pleases everyone in the organization, he must also absorb the displeasure, and sometimes severe hostility, of those who would have taken a different course.

A colleague recently summed up what my experience has taught me in these words: 'A good leader must be tough enough to win a fight, but not tough enough to kick a man when he is down.' This notion is not in the least consistent with humane, democratic leadership. Good human relations develop out of strength, not of weakness.

One of Douglas McGregor's students who acted as a joint editor of the collection of essays entitled *Leadership and Motivation* (1966) in which this passage appears was Warren

Bennis. The youngest US company commander in Europe at the end of the Second World War, Bennis also became a university president. It was he more than any other with his book *Leaders* (1985) who launched the revival of interest in organizational leaders. The major contribution of the new school lay in emphasizing the nexus between leadership and vision.

Those in the military field at such institutions as West Point and Sandhurst, with their own traditions of leadership, never abandoned the Qualities Approach. It reaches back to Xenophon, for he listed the qualities of an ideal leader as: *temperance, justice, sagacity, amiability, presence of mind, tactfulness, humanity, sympathy, helpfulness, courage, magnanimity, generosity* and *considerateness*.

At Sandhurst the basic list was derived from a lecture on leadership given there by General Slim. His qualities were: *courage, willpower, judgement, knowledge, flexibility of mind* and *integrity*. These also formed the substance of his lectures on leadership to management audiences. For his part, Montgomery mentioned with approval Aristotle's four leadership virtues: *justice, temperance, prudence* and *fortitude*.

My own view is that a leader should possess and exemplify the qualities expected or required in his or her field. So a military leader, for example, will need physical courage as well as the other characteristics of any good soldier. But there are some more generic leadership qualities, such as *enthusiasm* and *integrity* – the quality that makes people trust you – the combination of *toughness* or demandingness and *fairness, warmth* or humanity with *energy* and *resilience*.

This list is not exhaustive, for with leadership there are always facets of the diamond that catch the light in some individuals in certain circumstances and not in others. So you can always study the qualities of leaders and see – or see afresh – new facets. *Humour*, for example, not mentioned above, can be a powerful leadership quality. No one has the sum of all these contributory qualities, for the ideal leader is a concept not a person. But you should aim to develop the natural qualities that you have, which fall within the general flight path indicated earlier. If you try and fail, the good news is that you will tend to become more humble – and humility is a most useful leadership quality as well!

THE SITUATIONAL APPROACH

Enough has been said about the Situational Approach not to warrant more here. Suffice to say that in its classical form it lays more emphasis upon the technical or professional competence – in a word, knowledge – of the leader, than upon his or her qualities of personality or character (not that these are unimportant in the true classic tradition).

You may have noticed that General Slim put knowledge on his list. Speaking within the military context, then an all-male environment, this is what he had to say in his lecture on 'Leadership in Management', given in 1957 in Australia when he was Governor-General:

I said he must have knowledge. A man has no right to set himself up as a leader – or to be set up as a leader – unless he knows more than those he is to lead. In a small unit, a platoon say – or maybe a workshop gang – the leader should be able to do the job of any man in the outfit better than he can. That is a standard that should be required from all junior leaders. As the leader rises higher in the scale, he can no longer, of course, be expected to show such mastery of the detail of all the activities under him. A Divisional Commander need not know how to coax a wireless set, drive a tank, preach a sermon or take out an appendix as well as the people in his division who are trained to do those things. But he has got to know how long these jobs should take, what their difficulties are, what they need in training and equipment and the strain they entail. As the leader moves towards the top of the ladder, he must be able to judge between experts and technicians and to use their advice although he will not need their knowledge. One kind of knowledge that he must always keep in his own hands – is that of men.

Although one may question all of that last sentence, it certainly points to a more generic knowledge – a knowledge about human nature and how best people might work together in organizations – which is characteristically present in effective leaders. Whether or not that wider knowledge of human nature, of 'the human side of enterprise', knowing how to lead, is present in any given individual can be principally judged by their actions.

Knowing what to do in situations is partly a factor of technical/professional knowledge and partly a factor of knowledge about people (if those situations involve people, as in the case of leadership they invariably will). But two other factors – *intelligence* and *experience* – also come into the equation. In the Socratic concept of *knowledge*, you could say, *intelligence* and *experience* are in-built. That may be so, but it is worth artificially separating them out here for the sake of understanding.

As a general common-sense principle, a leader should be at least as intelligent as the average if not above average. As Ordway Tead wrote in *The Art of Leadership* (1935): 'What little scientific evidence there is above the consensus of observable facts seems to point to the truth that, *other qualities being equal*, the person of greater intelligence will probably make the better leader.'

Intelligence is the faculty of understanding. Mental alertness, problem-solving ability and keeping perception of relationships are all implicit in intelligence. Mental ability in this wider and more informal sense is obviously transferable than any specific technical know-how. As Tead continues:

> The few studies available indicate also that this higher intelligence factor in leaders correlates with *versatility*. The tentative conclusion seems to be that those capable of leading in one field are likely to be found potentially high in capacity to lead in several fields. The kind of eager, alert, outreaching mental quality which marks the leader predisposes him to use his powers in several directions.

Intelligence in this context includes the ability:

- To see the point
- To sense relationships and analogies quickly
- To identify the essentials in a complex picture
- To 'put two and two together'
- To find the salient factors in past experience, which are helpful in shedding light on present difficulties
- To be able to distinguish clearly between ends and means
- To appraise situations readily
- To see their significance in the total setting of present and past experience
- To get the cue as to the likely line of wise action

These overlap considerably, but taken together they offer an idea of the kind of intelligence we are talking about.

In the list above the interdependence of intelligence with experience is evident. Experience can be either experience of life in general, which of course only comes with age, or relevant experience to a given situation. Familiarity is based upon considerable actual practice. You have personally encountered, undergone or lived through situations not unlike the one now faced. By implication, this past immersion in a subject or field has resulted in superior understanding. Sometimes, however, gain in wisdom need not be suggested by the word so much as a piling-up of involvement. Marshal Saxe's donkey, it is said, went on twenty campaigns carrying his master's baggage, but learned nothing about the art of war.

The Greeks had a word for this combination of intelligence and experience in practical affairs – *phronesis*. It was translated into Latin as *prudentia* and thence into English as *prudence*. Essentially, *prudent* suggests action that is the outcome of wisdom gained by experience. The ability to govern and discipline oneself by the use of reason, sagacity or shrewdness in the management of affairs, prudence in the use of resources, caution or circumspection as to danger or risk – you can see why Aristotle placed *phronesis* among the 'Intellectual Virtues'. As prudence carries a slight overtone of restraint, a better translation of *phronesis* today is practical wisdom.

THE FUNCTIONAL APPROACH

My first encounter with the Functional Approach to leadership was on the receiving end. In 1953, a month or two into National Service, I was sent to the War Office Selection Board (WOSB) for it to determine whether or not I should be offered a commission as an officer. It was a fair, interesting and impressive experience, and I do not say that simply because I passed! Not that I understood all the theory behind it – nor, I suspect, did those officers who staffed it.

WOSBs, as they were known – the grandparent of all

assessment centres today – had been introduced in 1942 while the British Army was expanding rapidly from a few hundred thousand to some six million men and women. The traditional interview method of officer selection from the public schools was clearly not working effectively. The Adjutant-General of the day, Sir Ronald Adam, convened a working party of soldiers and psychologists in uniform who jointly designed the three-day selection process.

Dr Henry Harris, one of the psychologists involved from 1943 onwards, wrote a book on this remarkable innovation, entitled *The Group Approach to Leadership Testing* (1949). The essential problem, he wrote, was how to select the right man for the right group, given that small military groups, which would have to operate in the stress conditions of the battlefields, needed a leader who could function efficiently under stress:

> WOSB's answer was to test and evaluate him in the context of a small experimental group submitted to considerable time and problem stress, i.e. required to execute a difficult task against time. That which one sought to observe and evaluate one might call his group effectiveness, the sum total of his contribution to the group and its task.

Group effectiveness was broken down into *task functioning*, such as planning and organizing the available abilities, materials and time, and *group-cohesiveness functioning*, notably the ability to bind the group in the direction of the common task and to relate its members emotionally to each other and to the task. Also observed and noted was the ability of the candidate to withstand the effects of stress, which today we could call resilience. 'One selects and *tests* him *in* a group and *for* a group': that was the essential principle.

It is clear that in these early days the elements of the Functional Approach were available and put to use for leadership selection. In this thoughtful summary Henry Harris writes:

> One may suggest provisionally that leadership is the measure and degree of an individual's ability to influence – and be influenced by – a group in the implementation of a common task. This circumscribes three important aspects of leadership function: the *individual*, the *group* and the *task*; and indicates leadership as a functional relationship between these three basic variables.

Personally I hate war, necessary evil though it may sometimes be, and I am eternally grateful to those whose labours and sacrifices have removed the threat of it for most of us. Yet war is often the matrix of accelerated technological development, witness the computers and jet engines that emerged from the Second World War. The Functional Approach and its massive testing in the WOSB application is another such example.

My own work in the 1960s at Sandhurst could be interpreted as the application of the Functional Approach to the issue of *training* leaders as opposed to *selecting* them. The approach focused in a two-day practical course of exercises, group discussions, film and case study proved to be successful, and became widely adopted in the British Armed Services and overseas. Renamed 'Action-Centred Leadership' (ACL), it was introduced to industry by me, and more than one million managers and supervisors participated in the programme.

One key breakthrough that made this success possible was relating the three elements of 'need' – *task, group* (renamed *team*) and *individual* – in a simple diagram. As the Chinese proverb says: 'A picture is worth a thousand words.'

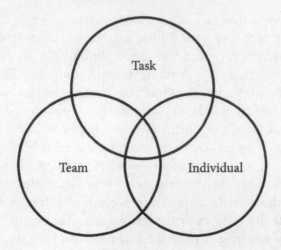

The interaction of areas of need

If you place a disc over the 'Task' circle in the figure above, it will immediately cover segments of the other two circles as well. In other words, lack of task or failure to achieve it will affect both team maintenance, for example increasing disruptive tendencies; it will also affect the area of individual needs, lowering member satisfaction within the group. Move the disc on to the 'Team' circle, and again the impact of a near-complete lack of relationships in the group on both task and individual needs may be seen at a glance.

Conversely, when a group achieves its task the degree of group cohesiveness and enjoyment of membership should go up. Morale, both corporate and individual, will be higher. And if the members of a group happen to get on extremely well together and find that they can work closely as a team, this will increase their work performance and also meet some important needs that individuals bring with them into common life.

These three interlocking circles therefore illustrate the

general point that each area of need exerts an influence upon the other two; they do not form watertight compartments.

Clearly, in order that the group should fulfil its task and be held together as a working team, certain functions will have to be performed. By 'function' in this context we mean any behaviour, words or actions that meet one or more spheres of 'need', or *areas of leadership responsibility* as they may also be called. Defining the aim, planning and encouraging the group, are examples of what is meant by the word 'function'. The box opposite shows other examples.

This three circle model also served as a framework for other satellite theories or models, such as Abraham Maslow's theory of a hierarchy of individual needs and the model that represented the different ways a leader could share a decision with a group or individual – starting with *telling* and becoming progressively more participative – seen as points on a decision-making continuum (for details of both see my other books in this series including *Effective Decision Making and Effective Leadership*). The general principle that emerges is that the more you share decisions the better, for the people involved will feel more committed to carrying them out. But there are natural factors – shortage of time, extent of knowledge and experience of the group or individual – which may limit how far you can go.

In summary, a leader is the sort of person with the appropriate *qualities* and *knowledge* – which is more than technical or professional – who is able to provide the necessary *functions* to enable a team to achieve its task and to hold it together as a working unity. And this is done not by the leader alone but by eliciting the contributions and willing cooperation of all involved. As Sir John Smyth, VC, wrote:

A good leader is someone whom people will follow through thick and thin, in good times and in bad, because

SOME KEY LEADERSHIP FUNCTIONS	
PLANNING	• Seeking all available information • Defining group task, purpose or goal • Making a workable plan (in the right decision-making framework)
INITIATING	• Briefing team on the aims and the plan • Explaining *why* aim or plan is necessary • Allocating tasks to group members • Setting team standards
CONTROLLING	• Maintaining group standards • Influencing tempo • Ensuring all actions are taken towards objectives • Keeping discussion relevant • Prodding group to action/decision
SUPPORTING	• Expressing acceptance of persons and their contribution • Encouraging team/individuals • Disciplining team/individuals • Creating team spirit • Relieving tension with humour • Reconciling disagreements or getting others to explore them
INFORMING	• Clarifying task and play • Giving new information to the group, keeping them 'in the picture' • Receiving information from the group • Summarizing suggestions and ideas coherently
EVALUATING	• Checking feasibility of an idea • Testing the consequences of proposed solution • Evaluating team performance • Helping team or individual to evaluate their own performance against standards

they have confidence in him as a person, his ability and
his knowledge of the job and *because they know they
matter to him.*

THE THREE CIRCLE MODEL IN PERSPECTIVE

The three circle Functional Leadership concept is now the best
known and most widely used leadership-development model
in the world. Many models and theories have come and gone,
but none other has been consistently employed in selection
and developments for over fifty years and has, in that time,
grown in reputation. As the English proverb says: 'Time tries
truth.' In this field, time does help to sift out the merely
ephemeral or fashionable so-called theories of leadership.

There are, however, two respects that have come to my
notice in that long period in which the three circle model is
not foolproof. First, the equal size of the three circles has led
a few tyro-leaders to assume that they always spend equal
time and energy on the task, team and individual. In fact, as
most people realize, one circle may be much 'larger' than
another in the sense that in some situations you may have to
focus mainly upon one area at the temporary expense of the
other two. A good leader may well redress the balance when
circumstances allow. But the three circle model is dynamic
rather than static; the shape or pattern is constantly changing.

Second, it has been argued that the model encourages
mediocrity in that it assumes a team that merely accom-
plishes a task given to it: it does not improve on the task or
come up with a better one. But this is a misconception, a
reading of something into the model that is not there. In
fact it encompasses the creative group or team that invents
its own task or chooses to transcend the already defined task
it has been given. Indeed, the degree of creativity in any one

of the three circles will – following the interactive principle – affect both the other circles. If, for example, you give a team a creative task to do, it will evoke the latent creativity in both group and individuals. If you introduce a highly creative person into the team, the task will be seen and approached in a more creative way and the group as a whole may well become more effective.

By the light of experience it now seems as if the three circle model is – in the sphere of leadership – the modest equivalent to Einstein's General Theory of Relativity. For it obeys Einstein's principle that: 'Everything should be made as simple as possible, but not more simple.' The model is simple and true, which means that it can never be simplistic or superficial.

LEVELS OF LEADERSHIP

Leadership exists on different levels. Thinking of organizations, there are three broad levels or domains of leadership:

Team The leader of a team of some ten to twenty people with clearly specified tasks to achieve.

Operational The leader of one of the main parts of the organization and more than one team leader are under one's control. It is already a case of being a leader of leaders.

Strategic The leader of a whole organization, with a number of operational leaders under one's personal direction.

A simple recipe for organizational success is to have effective leaders occupying these roles and working together in harmony as a team. This is simple enough to say: I am not implying that it is easy either to achieve or to maintain this state of affairs under the pressures of life today. But what is your alternative?

Within each broad level there may be subdivisions. The levels also overlap considerably. But the distinction is still worth making.

Sometimes, however, these three floor levels of the organizational house are disguised by the elaborate façade of hierarchy. A *hierarchy* (from Greek *hierus* meaning sacred) originally meant a ruling body of priests or clergy organized into orders or ranks, each subordinate to the one above. The Greek *archos* was a generic term for a man who was in authority over others: their leader. It comes from a verb, which means both to begin and to take the lead. Hence our English word-ending, *–archy*, which means government or leadership of or by an *arch*. An *archbishop*, for example, is the first or leader among bishops, whereas *monarchy* is rule by one person – a king or emperor.

In Greek phalanxes and Roman formations there were *archoi* of various names among the rank-and-file. But once battle was joined, the formations tended to disintegrate and the natural 'leaders of ten' emerged to rally and lead their comrades forward.

The foundation is the team leader, a truth that continues to evade many large organizations today. 'Ten soldiers wisely led will beat one hundred without a head,' wrote the Greek poet Euripides. A *decanus* in Greek and Latin was the leader of ten soldiers. From its use in monastic orders for a monk in charge of ten others, the word comes down to us in the form of dean – the dean of a cathedral or the dean of a university faculty. Our military equivalent is corporal, which derives, like captain, from Latin *caput*, head. *Chief*, coming from *chef*, the French for a head, has the same meaning.

Because as humans we stand erect, we tend to assume that a head is a hierarchical model: the head is on top so it is important. But look at most other animals: the head always goes first – it is the body's leader.

In war, tactical formation is no substitute for team leaders. General Slim once recounted a conversation on that very point:

> I remember a long time ago, when I was a very earnest young staff officer, a lot of us – even in those days we did a certain amount of work in the army – were studying how a battalion should be formed up to attack. We had all sorts of ideas and argued them with tremendous enthusiasm. Watching and listening was an elderly man, a very fine fighting soldier, and we turned to him and said: 'What do you think, sir?'
>
> 'Well,' he answered, 'I can tell you one thing. It does not matter what formation your battalion starts in – square, diamond, arrow, line, column, or squashing matchbox – it will always end up in the same formation – small groups rallying around the bravest men.' I have since seen a lot of battalions go into action, in all sorts of formations, but in the end they have always been like that – small groups round the natural leaders.

A team leader in action

A special correspondent representing the combined British Press writes from one of the beach-heads, dated Wednesday:

Down here on the beaches today I have been listening to stories of heroism at the first assault. The first men to hit the beaches were Commando units, and their boats were raked with mortar and machine-gun fire as they rode the surf into the assault area.

A young Commando corporal from one boat was seen by many of his comrades to sink to his knees half-way up a section of the beach towards a pill-box. He was quickly on his feet again and shouting: 'Come on mates,' rushed right into the mouth of the pill-box from which half a dozen machine guns were firing. He fell again in the doorway and this time did not get up. He had led his men right to the death and his body had more than fifty wounds in it. The ten Germans inside the pill-box surrendered to the survivors of that gallant assault.

The Times, 9 June 1944

Even a very large and globally widespread organization can exhibit in classic form the three levels of leadership. If you are a Roman Catholic, for example, in a Church that has millions of members throughout the world, there are only three leaders that come within your mental and spiritual compass: the parish priest, the diocesan bishop and the Pope as head of the Church. Of course there are other ranks and grades of clergy in the hierarchy but they do not obscure that essential three-level pattern. One of the strengths of the Catholic Church lies in the basic simplicity of its organization, worldwide though it is.

KEY POINTS: WHAT IS LEADERSHIP?

- There are three main approaches to understanding leadership, like paths converging towards the mist-shrouded summit of a mountain: Qualities, Situational and Functional. Each makes a vital contribution.
- A leader should personify the qualities expected in any worker in their field, as well as some of the more generic

attributes of a leader – for instance, enthusiasm, integrity, toughness and fairness, humanity, energy and resilience.

- As Socrates first pointed out, a leader should know his or her business. To that technical/professional knowledge must be added knowledge of human nature. Knowing what to do in situations calls for what the Greeks called *phronesis* or practical wisdom – a blend of intelligence and experience serviced by character.

- The Functional Approach integrates the other two in the 'breakthrough' model of the three circles – task, team and individual. The role of any leader can be defined by the model, and then further broken down for selection or training purpose into *functions*. There are a set of common *functions* – things you have to do – if these three overlapping areas of responsibility are to be met:

Defining the task	What are the purpose, aims and objectives? Why is this work worthwhile?
Planning	A plan answers the question of *how* you are going to get from where you are now to where you want to be. There is nothing like a bad plan to break up a group or frustrate individuals.
Briefing	The ability to communicate, to get across to people the task and the plan.
Controlling	Making sure that all resources and energies are properly harnessed
Supporting	Setting and maintaining organizational and team values and standards.
Informing	Bringing information to the group and from the group – the *linking* function of leadership.
Reviewing	Establishing and applying the success criteria appropriate to the field.

These are best called *leadership functions*. Together they constitute the *role* of a leader, but leadership is more than the sum of those parts.

- Which circle is dominant in the mind of a leader at any one time depends upon the circumstances. For the three cicles model is dynamic and not static. It does suggest, however, the need for a balance over the longer term.

- Leadership is discernible on three broad levels: team, operational and strategic. These constitute the natural hierarchy in all working organizations, although the levels overlap and may be subdivided in a variety of ways.

Keep your fears to yourself but share your courage with others.
Robert Louis Stevenson, Scottish novelist and poet

4

THE ROLE OF
STRATEGIC LEADER

'No one would have doubted his ability to reign
if he had never become emperor.'
Tacitus, Roman historian, speaking of Emperor Galba

We are now approaching the summit of the mountain. The
distinguishing characteristic of the strategic leadership level,
as we have seen, is that it implies responsibility for the *whole*
as contrasted to the *part*, be it large (operational) or small
(team). The three circle model, however, applies to organizations as well as teams. It is worth dwelling on this point
for a moment because it is not widely recognized. Functional
leadership is often – and wrongly – assumed to relate to
teams only.

UNDERSTANDING ORGANIZATION

To *organize* means arranging so that the whole aggregate
works as a unit, with each element having a proper function.
The Greek word *organon* meant literally 'that with which
one works' and is related to *ergon*, work. It also meant a tool

or instrument, especially a musical or surgical instrument. But it was also used figuratively to describe the parts of the human body that were regarded as instruments of sense of faculty.

That sense of something made deliberately for man's use carries over into our concept of an organization. The *-ation* at the end of these long Latin-derived words means the action or process itself, or the resulting condition: so an organization is what you get as a result of organizing, which in turn means systematic arranging for a definite purpose.

There is a useful distinction to be made between an *organization* and a *community*, though both are the products of humans imposing order on chaos. A community derives from the family, kindred group or tribe and has order through acceptance of common law and a form of government. Our nation states stand in this line of descent. Organizations, by contrast, are hunting parties at large. They are formed and developed with a particular form of work or – in the most general sense – task in mind.

You can eat apples, pears, grapes or bananas but you cannot eat *fruit*. For fruit is a generic and therefore abstract concept. In a similar vein, you can see and experience life in organizations like an army, church, government department, bank or computer company but you will never encounter *organization* as such, apart from its forms. You cannot see or touch it. It is an abstract concept too, like fruit.

Why bother with such an abstract concept? Because the world of organizations is extremely complex; organizations differ in size and shape, in purpose or function. Some are young and thrusting, others are old and venerable institutions. Not only does national culture colour them but they develop their own organizational cultures. Faced with this bewildering variety it is natural for the human mind to search for what is generic and common. It is a seeking of simplicity in the fact of apparent complexity but not for a purely academic end. For the concept of strategic leadership as at least theoretically a transferable art depends upon organizations having – beneath the surface – a generic unity. So organization is worth exploring further.

The only ways we can think about something as abstract as organizations is by analogy or metaphor. One of the oldest metaphors used to help us understand is the human body. An organization – any organization – is a form of a whole made up of interdependent parts. The essence of those two aspects – whole and parts – is generic; it is the essence of organization. The human body metaphor gives us some of our generic language about organization, such as *head* or *chief*, *corporate* and *member*.

THE THREE CIRCLE MODEL

If we widen the metaphor and think of the human *person* and not just the body, that suggests two ideas. First, just as each of us is unique and has our own distinctive personality, so groups – if they stay together – develop a *group personality*. And organizations, which are teams writ large, also form an *organizational personality* or corporate culture as it is commonly called. It finds expression in the behaviour typical in that group or organization. Remember, therefore, that every organization you encounter is unique and one of your first requirements as its strategic leader will be to be aware of that uniqueness.

Different though we all are as individual persons, we share some things in common, such as the attribute of personality itself. Most obviously, we all have needs – for food, drink and shelter, for example. Following that analogy, all organizations have three areas of need present in them:

- The need to accomplish the common task. Why is an organization formed? To achieve a task that an individual or small group cannot do on its own.
- The need to be held together and maintained as a working unity – a whole and not just a collection of discordant parts.
- The need that individuals bring with them into any organization.

Clearly we are back now to the three circle model – the great discovery that the three areas of 'need' in *any* organization will act upon each other in an inter-influential way for good or ill. Therefore the role of a strategic leader is to do for the *whole* what other leaders should accomplish for the parts.

THE RELATION OF THE WHOLE TO THE PARTS

Under the microscope, the abstract invisible *organization* that informs all the organizations you or I have ever known turns out to have an atomic structure – the three interacting areas of forces that I have called needs. As if in response to these needs a simple *hierarchy* of three levels of *leader* can be observed. By some subatomic work the six or seven main *functions* that compose their *roles* can also be mapped. So enormous strides have been made in the understanding of *organization*, though the many and various applications of that knowledge in the world of actual organizations lag far behind.

From the analysis it is clear that one major issue in all organization is *getting the right balance between the whole and the parts*.

Alfred P. Sloan who, along with Pierre DuPont, had an

immense influence on corporate organizations in the US saw this key issue in managerial teams. Writing in *My Years with General Motors* (1963), he expressed it thus: 'Good management rests on a reconciliation of centralization and decentralization, or "decentralization with coordinated control."' For 'centralization' read *whole* and for 'decentralization' read *part*. Sloan's solution, as he hinted in his last phrase, is a *both-and-one*: decentralization but maintaining some control from the centre.

That sounds simple, but in practice it is not easy to achieve. No formula exists, whatever the popular pundits or gurus with their quick-fix solutions may say. As a strategic leader you have to be able to think it out for yourself. As Sloan continued:

> There is no hard and fast rule for sorting out the various responsibilities and the best way to assign them. The balance which is struck ... varies according to *what is being decided, the circumstances of the time, past experience,* and the *temperaments and skills of the executive involved.*

The relation of the whole to the parts as a perennial issue applies in both *unitary* and *federal* organizations. For there are *unitary* organizations, the ones that resemble your body; and there are *federal* ones, which are more like your family. In the political field, federal (from the Latin *foedus*, a compact or league) set-ups are composed of political units that surrender their individual sovereignty to a central authority, but retain limited residuary powers of self-government. Power is distributed between that central authority and its constituent territorial units. The degree to which they are integrated varies from a *union*, where there is virtually one political identity, to a loose *federation* which functions more like an alliance whose members can choose to leave if they wish. You will be familiar with the debates raging in Europe about the nature of the European Union. Does having its own currency and military force constitute steps towards a strong federalist super-state on the model of the US?

Unitary organizations tend to resemble armies in that you can theoretically tell people what to do and they will do it. In modern jargon they are 'command and control organizations'. And in historical terms, as the Roman centurion put it simply to Jesus in Matthew 8:9: 'I am a man under authority, with soldiers under me; and I say to this one, "Go", and he goes, and to another, "Come", and he comes, and to my slave, "Do this", and he does it.'

In federal organizations it is all very different. As the federal leader you can lead but you cannot command. For example, in the Church of England – a federation of forty-three dioceses each headed by a bishop with its own diocesan synod and administration – the Archbishop of Canterbury supported by his brother Archbishop of York who presides over the northern of the two provinces and their new Archbishop's Council, can only make things happen by carrying the diocese with him.

Beneath the surface here you can identify the perennial and ever-present issue of the relations of the *whole* to the *parts*. That in turn is a reflection of the still deeper tensions between the values of *order* and *freedom*. They appear to be opposites but the true function of *order* is to create *freedom*.

Where *all* leaders – not just those at strategic levels – are committed to the whole as well as to their particular part, and where each fulfils his or her role with all the qualities of a good leader, the organization is dancing. The teamwork of the leaders produces an effect that is best described as *harmony* – the Greek word *harmos*, joint, also gives us words like *arm*. All the arms or parts move and work together in a pleasing and even graceful cooperation like the chords of a musical composition or dancers in a chorus-line.

In this respect a great orchestra is a strong metaphor illuminating that underlying concept of organization, which all organizations must express. The parts are the individual players, grouped together in four teams – strings, woodwind, brass and percussion, each with its own 'first' player or leader. In rehearsal and performance a conductor is the operational leader, whose conducting holds the teams together in an artistically expressive interpretation of the composer's score. The conductor – from the Latin word for one who leads people together or jointly – provides both direction in the performance and cohesion in the orchestra.

Yet an orchestra is a relatively small organization and a good conductor can establish rapport with all the players literally over the heads of the section leaders as well as with those playing solo parts. In very large organizations, say an army of hundreds of thousands, it is obviously much more difficult for the strategic leader to relate directly to people in that way but great leaders achieve just that.

In summary, three important things are common to organization in a generic sense – that which applies to *all* organizations as if they were manifestations of a platonic idea:

- The three interacting circles of 'need' apply in every instance, just as needs for food, security and recognition are common to us all.
- Every organization, like every individual person, is unique; it has a distinct group personality or corporate culture that is its generic fingerprints.
- The issue of the relation of the whole to the parts, the balance of order and freedom, is common to all.

It could be added, too, that all organizations are like fish: whether they are whale-sized or sprat-sized, they swim in the sea of society.

THE FUNCTIONS OF STRATEGIC LEADERSHIP

Although it has been a recent fashion to produce long lists of leadership 'competencies' – some as thick as telephone books – the essential requirements of a leader are simple. The core role at any level refracts into broad functions derived from the three circle model. The three general functions are:

The broad functions of strategic leadership

This role, of course, has to be fulfilled against a background of a society that has many continuities but is subject to a manner of changes that constantly impact on each of the three areas and the organization as a whole. Working from some first principles of organization, I think at present the

FUNCTIONS	KEY ELEMENTS
Providing direction for the organization as a whole	*Purpose/Vision/Values*
Getting strategy and policy right	*Strategic Thinking and Planning*
Making it happen	*Operational/Administration*
Organizing or reorganizing	*Organization Fitness to Situational Requirement*
Releasing the corporate spirit	*Energy, Morale, Confidence, Esprit de corps*
Relating the organization to other organizations and society as a whole	*Allies and Partners, Stakeholders, Government*
Developing tomorrow's leaders	*Teaching and leading the learning by example*

generic role of strategic leadership (or *strategia*) refracts into seven 'colours' or functions – in no order of importance:

What fits a person to fulfil this role? It is clearly a demanding and challenging one, even though there is professional staff at hand – sometimes in cohorts to help the strategic leader where the responsibilities are great.

Let us assume that the strategic leader has awareness, understanding and skill in the three circle model. Assume too that he or she knows their business. Take for granted as well personal leadership qualities such as enthusiasm, integrity, fairness, toughness, calmness, humanity and resilience. What is important next is the *mind* of the strategic leader as opposed to his or her heart and spirit.

INTELLIGENCE

The primary responsibility of the strategic leader is for the *whole* of the organization, as opposed to its *parts*, however large or significant they may be. And, by definition, a whole is more complex than a part. Add to this factor of complexity another: the positioning and relationship of the whole organization within a rapidly changing and highly complex social, political, economic and technological environment – and a global one at that. In order to fulfil effectively the strategic leadership role at that level, a person needs an above-average level of *intelligence*. Or, putting it another way, above-average intelligence is a necessary condition for a strategic leader but not a sufficient one. You may well fail without it but it is not a single guarantee of success. It is right that at a strategic level it is less easy for leaders today than it was – due to an increase in complexity – to make up for the absence of intelligence by persistence or dogged determination, or by integrity and friendliness, to offset their limitations in mental ability.

Of course the complexity was always there, for strategic leaders have always had to deal with a more complex task, a more complex group and more complex individuals in their top teams than leaders at lower levels in the hierarchy. But the nature and extent of change have certainly made things considerably more complex than the days when the river of life moved forward in a slower and more placid way.

The principle is clear: 'The general truth still stands out,' as Ordway Tead wrote over sixty years ago, 'that one should not assume a leadership role with which one's intelligence is not able to cope. No leader can [or should?] rise higher than his mentality will allow.' Here mentality (or intelligence) means a person's all-round effectiveness in activities that depend upon thought.

Themistocles

The intellectual powers required in a leader are exemplified by this Athenian statesman and general who lived in the fourth century B. C. Born of a father of no particular distinction and an alien mother, as a boy Themistocles showed unusual ability and application. Indeed, his career proved a point made by Pericles, that in Athens 'what counts is not membership of a particular class, but the actual ability which the man possesses.' As Thucydides wrote in his history of the war between Athens and Sparta, few surpassed Themistocles in practical wisdom:

> Themistocles was a man who showed an unmistakable natural genius; in this respect he was quite exceptional, and beyond all others deserves our admiration. Without studying a subject in advance or deliberating over it later, but using simply the intelligence that was his by nature, he had the power to reach the right conclusion in matters that have to be settled on the spur of the moment and do not admit of long discussions, and in estimating what was likely to happen, his forecasts of the future were always more reliable than those of others. He could perfectly well explain any subject with which he was familiar, and even outside his own department he was still capable of giving an excellent opinion. He was particularly remarkable at looking into the future and seeing there the hidden possibilities for good or evil. To sum him up in a few words, it may be said that through force of genius and by rapidity of action this man was supreme at doing precisely the right thing at precisely the right moment.

As a young man Themistocles fought at Marathon, the battle in which the Persian invasion of Greece by Darius was defeated. But he foresaw that the Persians would be back. He persuaded his fellow Athenians to build a fleet. There was not a day to spare, for the Persians returned under Xerxes thirsting for revenge. Themistocles showed his greatness as a leader by abandoning Athens to the invaders, concentrating the Greek fleet at Salamis and, by a clever stratagem, tricking the Persian fleet into attacking his triremes (ancient Greek warships) in harrow straits where it was utterly defeated.

I listed some of the aspects of intelligence in Chapter 3 (page 63). Especially important in strategic leadership, is the ability to step back from the complexity of detail and to see the 'wood for the trees' or 'the whole picture', so that its simple essentials or salient features stand out. Today this faculty is sometimes called 'taking the helicopter view', though it is no good going up in the metaphorical helicopter unless you have a trained analytical eye and some competence as a map-maker in your field.

Although Field Marshal Montgomery lacked some elements of *phronesis*, he excelled in this aspect of practical intelligence. Sticking to the strategic level of thought meant ruthlessly standing back from the complexity of the detail, except where detail was important enough to warrant the strategic leader's attention. In a lecture on 'Military Leadership' to the University of St. Andrew's in 1945, Montgomery made this point with characteristic clarity and vigour:

No man can be a great military leader unless he has the ability to cut through overlying difficulties, and to see clearly the few essentials in any problem with which he is faced. In any problem there are never more than a few essentials which are vital *to that problem*. These must be grasped out of the mass of details and must never be lost sight of. If in battle a commander loses sight of the few essentials that matter, he will suffer defeat.

But to see the essentials clearly he must not himself get

too immersed in detail. Every great commander has had a
chief of staff whose main task was the mastery of detail,
thus leaving the master free to tackle the essentials of the
problem together with those details, and only those details,
which were vital to that problem. For though there is
much detail with which a commander cannot and must
not bother himself, it is interesting to note that every great
commander has always concerned himself with certain of
the details of his problems. Napoleon and Wellington are
two good cases in point.

Strategy entails seeing the big picture and working on a large
canvas. But pictures are made up of details. When Monet
stepped back from a giant picture of waterlilies and then
stepped forward to touch in a spot of colour with the tip of
his brush, that attention to detail mattered. The art is to
know which details should concern you and which are best
left to your staff. Do not, like Admiral Beatty, check every
officer's mess bill in the fleet!

'Too much intellect is not necessary in war,' Napoleon
once wrote to his brother Joseph. 'Probably the most desirable attribute of all,' or so he told Emmanuel Las Cases, the
French historian who accompanied him into exile on St.
Helena, 'is that a man's judgement should be above the
common level. Success in war is based upon prudence, good
conduct, and experience.'

This generic strand in practical wisdom – Napoleon called
it prudence – of seeing things as they really are, not distorted
by wishful thinking or unhinged by false assumptions, or
restricted by a tunnel vision, 'he believed he had to an extraordinary degree.' He once remarked to General Gourgaud
that 'the one [quality] that distinguishes me the most, *is to
see the entire picture distinctly'*.

At Waterloo, Napoleon lost the day – just – to a general

who also shared this attribute. 'Wellington's real gift was transcendent common sense,' wrote military historian J. W. Fortescue, 'the rare power (shared also by Marlborough) of seeing things as they are, which signifies genius.' It is a comment that reminds me of the Spanish saying, *El sentido común es el menos común de los sentidos* – 'common sense is the least common of the senses'. To possess it to an above-average level is essential in a leader.

The ability to see the realities of a situation as a whole in this way sounds more like common sense than anything requiring intelligence. But remember that I said you do not have to be brilliant!

This clarity of freshness of vision – seeing the situation steadily as a whole with all its complex elements but also discerning its essentials – calls for what the Japanese call the *sunao* mind. Konosuke Matsushita, one of the most celebrated Japanese business leaders of the last century, strove for it all his life, as his close associate Toru Yamaguchi informed me:

> The *sunao* mind or the untrapped mind is calm and highly adaptable. It enables its owner to free himself of preconceived notions so that he can see things as they are. Managers who don't have the *sunao* mind are often swayed by their own interests in decision making, inevitably leading to corporate failure. Since managers, just like everyone else, are creatures of habit and prejudice, they have to cultivate the *sunao* mind to judge the situation accurately and lead the way to corporate success. Konosuke always said that cultivating the *sunao* mind is important, and that it wasn't easy, but he continued to his final days the constant work of developing it.

This freedom from preconceived notions, from subconscious assumptions and wishful thinking, is one of the marks of a person with the degree of *phronesis* required at all strategic leadership levels. There are countless examples of bad strategic decisions resulting from a failure to look at the world with a steady, unself-centred and dispassionate *sunao* mind, seeing it as it is and not as one would wish it to be. 'Without it,' Konosuke Matsushita wrote, 'one can enjoy neither genuine success in management nor genuine happiness in life.'

IMAGINATION

Themistocles exemplified *phronesis* – 'doing precisely the right thing at the right time' – but he also possessed another mental power valuable in a strategic leader – imagination. This is more highly desirable than essential, for others may well have creative ideas or imaginative suggestions. You do not have to be a creative thinker in the sense of being a person who reached valuable new combinations of ideas. But strategic leaders need imagination to see new possibilities in the present or the future. They should also be leaders in innovation – the process of bringing those valuable new ideas to the marketplace or community in the shape of new products or services because for most organizations today innovation is strategically important. Nor must one expect from a strategic leader who lacks imagination that priceless gift in any organization – vision.

Imagination refers to the mind's power to call up images, to picture or conceive things that are not actually before the eye or within the experience. And so it may apply to the representation of what is remembered, or of what has never been experienced in its entirety, or indeed of what is actually non-existent. For as humans we have this extraordinary and unique faculty to consider actions or events not yet in existence.

Imagination is linked to *phronesis* in so far as the latter includes the power to *foresee* – to see some development beforehand, as Themistocles foresaw what the Persians would return to invade Greece again. 'Forewarned, forearmed', says the proverb. Such a strategic leader will then *anticipate* the foreseen development – responding mentally to it and taking action before it happens. Foresight of this nature, however, may simply be knowledge derived from ordinary reason and experience, either at the conscious level or subconsciously through the process of information gathering, analysing and synthesizing that we call *intuition*. In other words, it is not creative.

Creativity is about bringing something into existence that did not exist before. Whatever the merits of this book, it did not exist until I committed my ideas to paper. We are *synthesizing* all the time – a word that means in Greek 'putting together' as opposed to *analysing*, separating. But we do not usually describe that as being creative unless the raw material and the finished product are very different. We then recognize that imaginative skill of a rare order – which belongs to an artist – has been at work.

Creative, imaginative, ingenious, inventive, original, resourceful – all the words apply to the active, exploratory mind and to its products, describing creators or creations that employ ordinary materials in extraordinary ways. *Creative* suggests the entire process whereby things that did not exist are conceived, given form, and brought into being.

On this spectrum, it is worth noting, an effective military strategic leader – a *strategos* or general – will certainly need to be *resourceful* – solving his problems despite limitation, finding whatever means are available and adapting them to his ends. He should also be *ingenious* in devising those stratagems that surprise, mislead or trick the enemy. But it is not a form of strategic leadership that calls for an *imaginative* mind – at least it did not in the past – still less for a *creative* one. A great general may create a fine army out of a rabble or create high morale out of despair, but no one pretends that war itself is anything but destructive – an evil if somewhat necessary one. In the majority of strategic roles, however, there is a clear and ever stronger call for imagination and creativity as well as practical wisdom.

HUMILITY

In his book on ethics Aristotle placed *phronesis* among the 'Intellectual Virtues', as it played a vital part in guiding a person to what is good or right conduct. Humility does not accompany it, which is surprising when you consider that its opposite, *hubris* – pride or arrogance – and its consequences are the stuff of Greek tragedies. What claim does humility have to be numbered among the intellectual virtues of an excellent strategic leader?

Humility is by origin a religious concept. The excessive self-confidence of *hubris* was interpreted as a form of insolence against the gods, who in Greek tragedy redress the balance by humiliating the offender. In the biblical tradition humility is the result of seeing God. In our more secular age it takes the form of having a sense of one's relative insignificance before something infinitely greater and better. You may know that you are very good, even the best in your field – humility does not imply lack of self-confidence or belief in yourself – but measured against the source and sum of all reality, what are you?

Because humility is a reflection, like the light of the moon, it is pointless to try to gauge your own degree of humility. If you feel that you are humble already compared to others you will be tempted to congratulate yourself, and pride comes on stage again! But you can see humility in the actions or words of others, providing they are sincere and not put on for the sake of show. Sir Isaac Newton, one of the great scientists of all time, once said:

> I do not know what I may appear to the world, but to myself I seem to have been only like a boy playing on the seashore, and diverting myself in now and then finding a smoother pebble or a prettier shell than ordinary, whilst the great ocean of truth lay all undiscovered before me.

Nor would Newton accept the fame thrust upon him. 'If I have seen further,' he wrote to the natural philosopher Robert Hooke in 1975, 'it is by standing on the shoulders of giants.'

Humility – a test of greatness

'I believe the first test of a truly great man is his humility. I do not mean by humility, doubt of his own power, or hesitation in speaking his opinions; but a right understanding of the relation between what *he* can do and say, and the rest of the world's sayings and doings. All great men not only know their business, but usually know that they know it, and are not only right in their main opinions, but they usually know that they are right in them; only, they do not think much of themselves on that account. Arnolfo knows he can build a good dome at Florence; Albrecht Dürer writes clearly to one who had found fault in his work, "It could not have been done better"; Sir Isaac Newton knows that he has worked out a problem or two that would have puzzled anybody else; – only they do not expect their fellow-men therefore to fall down and worship them; they have a curious under-sense of powerlessness, feeling that the greatness is not *in* them, but *through* them; that they could not do

or be anything else than God made them. And they see something Divine and God-made in every other man they meet, and
are endlessly, foolishly, incredibly merciful.'

John Ruskin, *Modern Painters* (1843)

In the Western tradition leadership is associated with strong
self-confidence and a powerful egotism – breeding-grounds
for the kind of *hubris* that the world witnessed in Hitler,
Mussolini and Stalin. Although Montgomery was a Christian
by belief, he was not untouched by arrogance as a leader.
T. E. Lawrence (on whose life the film *Lawrence of Arabia*
was based) was not noted for humility either, though he was
aware of the problem and welcomed humiliation – even
created his own – like the hero of a Greek tragedy. As far as
I know, the word humility was never applied to him.

Yet part of the effectiveness of three of the great Second
World War generals – Slim, Alexander and Eisenhower – lay
in the very fact that they possessed the personal grace and
intellectual virtue of humility, as their biographers testify.
My own conversations with Slim and Alexander left me with
this impression as well. General Sir John Glubb, as Glubb
Pasha and Commander-in-Chief of the Arab Legion in which
I served, was the only general I have come to know really
well personally. A deeply religious man, Glubb had a transparent humility about him.

'Humility must always be the portion of any man who
receives acclaim earned in the blood of his followers and the
sacrifices of his friends,' said Eisenhower. It was a quality he
regarded as essential in a leader:

A sense of humility is a quality I have observed in every
leader who I have deeply admired. I have seen Winston
Churchill with humble tears of gratitude on his cheeks as

he thanked people for their help to Britain and the Allied cause.

My own conviction is that every leader should have enough humility to accept, publicly, the responsibility for the mistakes of the subordinates he has himself selected and, likewise, to give them credit, publicly, for their triumphs. I am aware that some popular theories of leadership hold that the top man must always keep his 'image' bright and shining. I believe, however, that in the long run fairness and honesty, and a generous attitude towards subordinates and associates, pay off.

A good strategic leader will certainly accept complete personal responsibility if the decision he or she has made leads to failure. He or she will not 'pass the buck' to their colleagues or subordinates. After the failure of his first attack on Quebec, General Wolfe wrote: 'The blame I take entirely upon my shoulders and I expect to suffer for it. Accidents cannot be helped. As much of the plan as was defective falls justly on me.'

Eisenhower also shouldered the responsibility of failure. The weather conditions in the first few days of June 1944 caused his Air Commander to argue for further postponement of the invasion of Europe. After consultation with his generals and specialist advisers, Eisenhower himself took the momentous decision to take the risk and go ahead on 6 June 1944. Before the invasion fleet set out he wrote this press release, to be used if necessary:

Our landings have failed and I have withdrawn the troops. My decision to attack at this time and place was based upon the best information available. The troops, the Air and the Navy did all that bravery and devotion to duty could do. If any blame or fault is attached to the attempt it is mine alone.

Hitler exemplified the opposite side of the coin – irresponsibility. He persistently blamed the failure of his military plans upon the incompetence of his subordinates or their lack of willpower, while taking for himself the credit of the early successes. When the roof fell in Hitler castigated the German people for letting him down. He could neither see nor face his ultimate responsibility as leader.

Yet why is humility an *intellectual* virtue, as I have suggested it is? To accept that one may have been wrong after a decision and to accept the consequences is only one aspect of humility. To be open to others and their ideas before a decision means that you do not believe you are a genius who alone knows what to do – this is an equally important facet of humility. As the Scottish proverb says: 'The clan is greater than the chief.' A chief who believes this, is more likely to consult the clan and listen to their ideas. As author G. K. Chesterton said, 'It is always the secure who are humble.'

The principal contribution of humility to the mind of a strategic leader is that it signifies a marked lack of self in mental perception and calculations. Self is like an over-present shadow, it can obscure the clarity of the *sunao* or untrapped mind. In the original metaphor, to see God is to see reality as it is and all else including self in the blinding light of that sun. Putting it another way, if you and I could but see reality as it is – not just that which presents itself to our senses – we should reflect it as humility. And the more humble we are, the more likely it is that we shall see life and its changing situations and other people as they really are. Humble people are standing in front of their own shadows. They see clearly relations and proportions with the scheme of things.

'If you lack humility,' said James Blyth, a former chairman and chief executive of Boots, in a lecture on leadership, 'you are not a leader, not perhaps even a true person.' Blyth suggested that humility as a leader means:

- You acknowledge the common bond of humanity
- You accept that you are less than perfect
- You are willing to listen
- You have the resilience to try again

He quoted Peter Drucker: 'The leader of the past knows how to tell; the leader of the future will know how to ask.' A belief in oneself is not arrogance, he continued, but more confidence in that part of one's self that 'looks on tempests and is never shaken'. It is the ability to be closely in touch with the passing show, but not embroiled in it.

THE ANATOMY OF WISDOM

Wisdom outranks all other words – discernment, discrimination, judgement, sagacity and sense – when it comes to denoting mental qualities that have to do with the ability to understand situations, anticipate consequences and make sound decisions. For it suggests a rare combination of discretion, maturity, keenness of intellect, broad experience, extensive learning, profound thought and compassionate understanding. In its wider application, wisdom implies the highest and noblest exercise of the faculties of moral nature as well as of the intellect. In the slightly narrower compass of *phronesis*, wisdom can be analysed into three elements: *intelligence*, *experience* and *goodness*.

> Experience is by industry achiev'd
> And perfected by the swift course of time.

Apart from this vocational experience of which Shakespeare wrote in *The Two Gentlemen of Verona*, a broader experience of life is needed. Matched with intelligence, which I have sketched in here, the two work together like two eyes joined in sight. But why *goodness*?

The Greeks sensibly had two different words for good – *kalos* (skilled in, proficient at) and *agathos* (good in the moral sense). Originally, in Homeric times, *agathos* described how a man discharged his functions as king or warrior, judge or shepherd. To inquire if a Homeric nobleman was *agathos* meant was he courageous, wise and kingly? In other words, did he fight, manage and rule with success? Virtue or normal excellence referred to his art or skill in performing his socially allotted role. Later, *agathos* came to refer not to the qualities required to fulfil a role but to certain human qualities we call *goodness*.

Something of that original sense remains in the leadership context. For *integrity* and being *just* or fair are essential leadership qualities but both are also moral virtues. Therefore it is not strictly true that you can be a *good* leader without being a *leader for good*. Integrity, from the Latin *integer*, whole, implies a moral soundness and unity created by adherence to values as if outside oneself, notably truth. So integrity is close to honesty. They always breed trust. And what is more strategically important in all human relations than trust? 'Trust being lost,' wrote the Roman historian Livy, 'all the social intercourse of men is brought to nought.'

The element of *goodness* in wisdom could almost be described as *character*. By saying that a person has character (as opposed to personality and temperament) we mean that he or she has:

- A conception of what they should be and what others may rightly expect of them
- Principles that they will not be likely to betray
- Loyalties and commitments of an enduring kind
- Firmness when subject to attractive temptations

- Responsibility for their own actions and an expectation that others will be responsible too
- A sense of the reality of moral values, so that they are not a matter of personal preference

Character, from the name of the Greek tool used for engraving on stone or metal, consists of the attributes or features that mark out an individual. In this context, it applies more specifically to the aggregate of moral qualities by which a person is judged, apart from his or her intelligence, competence or special talents.

Why *goodness*? Because many of the decisions that will face you as a strategic leader will have a moral dimension to them. If you lack wisdom – intelligence, experience and goodness – your judgement will be fatally impaired. Not to know right from wrong as a leader is worse than not knowing port from starboard. A ship with such a morally blind leader at the helm is bound to crash into the rocks.

KEY POINTS: THE ROLE OF STRATEGIC LEADER

- An organization is the product of the activity of *organizing*. It is an instrument designed or evolved for a purpose and it can be best understood in terms of that purpose, the reason for its existence.
- Although we only know organizations, it is possible to think of human organization in the abstract. It has three elements, which are found genetically and generically in all working organizations:
  1. The three circle model – the interaction of task, group and individual.
  2. Being human, organizations always manifest a group

personality or culture that distinguishes one from another, even in the same social setting and field of enterprise.

3. The relation of the whole to the parts – order and freedom – is a fundamental issue in organization.

- The leadership role has evolved in response to the three interlocking areas of need. At strategic level the broad functions of achieving the task, building the team and developing the individual which constitute it, can be broken down further into seven generic functions, like light refracted into seven colours of the rainbow:

Providing direction for the organization as a whole

Getting strategy and policy right

Making it happen

Organizing or reorganizing

Releasing the corporate spirit

Relating the organization to other organizations and society as a whole

Developing tomorrow's leaders

- Strategic leadership differs not in kind but in magnitude of issues and scale of complexity encountered. It calls for a commensurate level of what the Greeks called *phronesis*, practical wisdom. 'A leader is not so much clever,' said Henry Kissinger, 'as lucid and clear-sighted.'
- As distinct from *phronesis*, the intellectual qualities of being imaginative and creative are desirable if not essential.
- Humility may seem an unlikely virtue in a leader but who wants to work for an arrogant chief executive? It contributes to the mental clarity of a thinker by reducing subjectivity.
- Wisdom – the mind of a *wita*, leader – is composed of

three elements: intelligence, experience and goodness. Character matters in all true leadership, not least at strategic level where it can be most under siege.

These are hard times in which a genius would wish to live.
Great necessities call forth great leaders.
        Abigail Adams, writing to Thomas Jefferson (1790)

PART TWO

LEADING THE WAY

PART TWO

5

THE FIRST HUNDRED DAYS

'A good beginning makes a good ending.'
English proverb

'I may be accused of rashness, but not of sluggishness,' Napoleon once told Marshal Berthier. Escaping from prison on Elba with a few aides, he landed in France and he won over the troops sent to arrest him, marched at their head into Paris, ejected the restored French king, resumed his imperial authority, reorganized the government, regrouped the *Grande Armée* and fought the decisive Battle of Waterloo. It almost came off – Wellington always described the battle as a close run thing – but in fact those three months of dynamic activity only led Napoleon back into a second exile on the tiny island of St. Helena in the middle of the Atlantic.

'A hundred days, sire, have elapsed since the fatal moment when Your Majesty was forced to quit your capital in the midst of tears,' begins the address of Count de Chambord, the prefect, after the signing of the abdication. This is the origin of our phrase 'The First Hundred Days' – in Napoleon's case the days between 20 March 1815 when he reached Paris and 28 June, the date of the second restoration of Louis XVIII.

'Let me assert my firm belief that the only thing we have
to fear is fear itself,' declared President Franklin D. Roosevelt in a ringing voice during his First Inaugural Address on
a chilly day in March 1933. Like a general taking over a
dispirited army, Roosevelt set about changing the 'atmosphere' of America so that it reflected his own confident,
positive and forward-looking spirit. His first one hundred
days, when he initiated the major recovery measures of what
he called the New Deal for America, did much to bring
about that change of mood. America awoke the morning
after the address feeling that an optimistic and constructive
leader was now at the helm of its fortunes.

Why do the first one hundred days create such an opportunity for strategic leaders? The answer is that most organizations have an established *status quo*, an existing state of
affairs. People know the familiar geography: what is important, where influence lies, what ideas are likely to be
accepted, who has prestige, how things are done, what
enhances one's career. They know where the land mines are.
The arrival of a new chief executive unbalances all this for
an all-too-brief period. Everything is temporarily up in the
air; nothing can be taken for granted and expectations of
change are high. There is a willingness to listen and learn, a
tacit agreement to suspend judgement and to give the newcomer the chance to show some leadership. It is the honeymoon period. Now or never. As Shakespeare wrote in *Julius
Caesar*:

> We, at the height, are ready to decline.
> There is a tide in the affairs of men,
> Which, taken at the flood, leads on to fortune;
> Omitted, all the voyage of their life
> Is bound in shallows and in miseries.
> On such a full sea are we now afloat,

And me must take the current when it serves,
Or lose our ventures.

Used well, this unique opportunity to challenge the *status quo* provides the new strategic leader with the chance to initiate a new order. Changes that you wish to make across the whole organization can be identified and signposted. What begins to be clear is what legacy you wish to leave behind you, the organization as it will be at the end of your last one hundred days – whenever that will be. If the new order is not established and does not start to settle in during or within reach of that short but critical first period, what happens? Yes, you are right, the old order reasserts itself. The organization is then moving quickly upon what poet Keats called 'the journey homewards to habitual self'.

To use this time well you, as the new strategic leader, need to have a clear picture of what you are trying to achieve and how you are going to go about it. Remember the military maxim: *Time spent on reconnaissance is seldom wasted*. Find out as much as you can about the organization. Talk to some of the key people. Make some visits. Formulate some working hypotheses – they are no more than that. Then you will be able to 'hit the deck running'.

THE FIRST CHALLENGE TO YOUR PRACTICAL WISDOM

'There are no precise or determined rules,' Napoleon declared. 'Everything depends on the character that nature has given to the general, on his qualities, his shortcomings, on the nature of the troops, on the range of firearms, on the season and on a thousand other circumstances which are never the same.' So the commander-in-chief has to think for himself, 'guided by their own experience or genius'. You may not be a genius but you certainly have an above-average degree of what, as we have seen, Napoleon called prudence – our old friend *phronesis*. Probably the most desirable attribute of all in a strategic leader, or so he told Las Cases, 'is that a man's judgement should be above the common level'. By prudence, incidentally, Napoleon did not mean that a good general should be cautious in the conduct of affairs. *Au contraire*: a good general 'must be slow in deliberation and quick in execution'. Whenever Napoleon used the word prudence he meant the exercise of intelligence and experience before making decisions, careful management and presence of mind. 'But all that will be of little use to him,' he warned, 'if he does not have the sacred fire in the depths of his heart, this driving ambition which alone can enable one to perform great deeds.'

You can see that Napoleon was not a man to waste the opportunities of those first hundred days. Success may have eluded him but he cannot be faulted for giving it less than his all. How about you?

Remember those words, 'slow in deliberation and quick in execution'. Don't rush in where the proverbial angels fear to tread. Take your time. Listen and observe, give your mind time to weigh things up in its own way; and test out your provisional decisions on those whom you can trust before you go public. But leave people in no doubt that within a limited period of time – it may not be the hundredth day – you will either be placing your seal on the present *status quo* or introducing change. 'What do you have in mind?' you will be asked. 'Wait and see,' you should reply. A little suspense does an organization no harm at all, providing you do not prolong it unnecessarily.

Setting a deadline, even if it is in your own diary, inoculates you against any tendency to procrastinate. The sheer unexpected complexity of things can propel you into an endless orbit of discussions, meetings – and more meetings – with the prospect of ever reaching conclusions and making decisions, which lead to action receding over the horizon. Before you know it's happened, the jungle of the *status quo* has reclaimed the clearing that your arrival made. It's back to business as usual.

For those who enjoy intellectual debate and who can easily be seduced into endless discussion it is worth taking on board the advice of President Woodrow Wilson – himself temperamentally inclined that way – to anyone in an executive strategic leadership position:

> In an executive job we intellectuals are dangerous, unless we are aware of our limitations and take measures to stop our everlasting disposition to think, to listen, not to act. I made up my mind long ago, when I got into my first executive job, to open my mind for a while, hear everybody who came to me with advice, information – what you will – then, some day, the day when my mind felt like deciding, to shut it up and act. My decision might be right; it might be wrong. No matter, I would take a chance and do – something.

For in the conduct of affairs any decision is better than no decision. You only have to be 80 per cent right. In real life as much depends upon the way you execute decisions as upon the decision itself. Generals such as Napoleon and Wellington were well aware of this fact, and did not delay decisions beyond the time when they needed to be made – whatever the shortfalls in information. The same principle applies in business, at least according to Percy Barnevik, a former Chairman of the ABB group of 1,200 companies, when it was the world's largest single supplier to the electricity industry:

> I would say that in any business decision 90 per cent of success is execution, 10 per cent strategy. And of that 10 per cent, only 2 per cent is really analysis and 8 per cent is guts to make uncomfortable decisions ... The question is, how do you mobilize people? How do you make 25,000 managers move like a big army? It doesn't matter so much if you move in the right direction or not, as long as you move. I tell people that if we make one hundred decisions and seventy turn out right, that's good enough.

I think the most difficult situation you will face is an organization where you get the feeling as you go round that everybody reckons they're doing all right. This is the hardest organization in which to bring about change.

These organizations tend to be ones that have been around quite a long time and are doing reasonably well and may have no obvious crisis looming, yet you know that if they just continue on that plateau the whole thing will erode. It's an interesting point whether or not as a strategic leader you need to introduce change for change's sake – like an unnecessary reorganization or selling the head office – just to wake up the organization.

Organizational complacency – or worse, corporate arrogance – is the deadliest enemy you will face as a strategic leader. If that is your fate, you must put on your prophet's mantle and go out on the highways and byways to proclaim high and low within the organization that it is *not* the best. Produce evidence, if need be, to support your case at every point. In this way you will plough the frost-bound hardened earth into furrows with the iron-tipped ploughshare of truth, ready for the seeds of change. The true leaders in the organization will know what you are talking about, not to mention its staff who face the daily realities of the business. As Sir John Harvey-Jones, former Chairman of ICI and TV business guru, once said:

> Everyone knows at any given moment which is the best company in its field. Not necessarily in terms of size or profits, though it could be. I mean the best in bringing new products, market sensitivity, presence, range, quality, how we deal with our people, ethical, environmental and safety standards – all of these things.

Only *phronesis*, practical wisdom – yours and other people's will tell you what potential there is in an organization to change for the better. Perhaps you and it will not know before you try. By the end of the first hundred days you should have received your own marching orders. A test is to ask, 'What would be my number one regret if I had to leave without achieving it?' and its corollary, 'What is the one thing that could derail that, now or in the future?'

KEY POINTS: THE FIRST HUNDRED DAYS

- You will never have a second chance to make a good first impression in an organization. It is worth giving some time and thought to evolve your personal strategy during those critical first three months in office.
- The arrival of a new strategic leader always opens the door – or pushes it further open – for change. The *status quo* is on trial. A new order may emerge. Expectations may be high, which fuels the energy for overcoming inertia and making positive changes.
- First you've got to understand thoroughly how the existing

system is working. Having come in as a new chairman or chief executive there is a window of opportunity and you have to make use of that, so it is a question of judgement and how quickly you can act.

- You may want to signal quite early that you think there are changes you will want to make, but make it absolutely clear that you're prepared to listen to what everyone else has to say. You're going to have to carry people with you, but you should be absolutely firm. Find out, listen, act.

- Get a grasp of the organization by getting around, meeting people and getting a feel for the actual business. If an organization is on the move, you certainly want to do any research you can to find out in which direction it is going.

- The other issue is relationships. You're going to have to work with people as individuals and collectively as a team. The role of the strategic leader includes getting the best of that collective group. This is going to take time but one of the first things to do is to try to establish some sort of personal link with people in the business.

- Think of that legacy, what you want to leave behind. As one chief executive of a company said, 'There is nothing more important than to leave behind an organization that feels confident of its future and feels like a winner.'

We must obey the greatest law of change. It is the most powerful law of nature.

Edmund Burke, Irish statesman and author

6

BUILDING THE TOP TEAM

'But of a good leader, who talks little,
When his work is done, his aim fulfilled,
They will all say "We did this ourselves."'
Lao Tzu (third century B. C.)

Teamwork at the top – individuals working in harmony together towards a common end – gives an organization an enormous strength. It sounds so simple and so obvious but it seems strangely difficult to achieve. Organizations lacking in it exhibit some well-known symptoms: intrigue, politicking and backbiting. Much of their energy is turned inwards upon itself in these internal feuds, clashes of ego and turf-wars. A knock-on effect in the organization can always be felt, like earth tremors spreading out from the epicentre. 'When the elephants fight, the grass gets trampled down,' as the African proverb puts it.

How do you achieve teamwork at the top? In this chapter I shall identify some of the areas of team composition and team maintenance that you should consider carefully. This is the necessary prelude before making any changes. The first area to look at is your own role.

WHAT IS YOUR OWN ROLE?

Let's assume, at least as far as Part Two of this book is concerned, that you are in a strategic leadership role or, in other words, you're the leader of a discrete organization. Is your leadership of the whole vested in you alone, or do you share the overall responsibility with a colleague? In British business terminology, are you chairman of the board *and* chief executive (officer) or managing director? Or do you hold only one of these roles?

Splitting the strategic leadership role may seem odd but there are two principal arguments for doing so. First, especially in a very large organization, there is too much work for one person to do on their own. Second, good corporate governance demands it. Since, in Lord Acton's well-known words, 'power tends to corrupt, and absolute power corrupts absolutely', the chief executive should be monitored by a yet more senior leader, who chairs the board of directors, governors, trustees or the like – the chairman, say, supported by some non-executive directors.

The counter-argument is the advantages of what the military call unity of command. Moreover, in some fields – whatever the workload – it is impractical to divide the top job. You cannot have two Popes. If one person is in charge, and that person has the necessary authority and power to act, then in theory at least, decisions get made more promptly and change can be more easily implemented. Not that the history of dictators always bears out this claim. Certainly strategic leadership without the substance of the power to act, hedged in by only the minimum restrictions, becomes a most frustrating business. Unlike the proverbial gift-horse, you should always look a strategic leadership role very carefully in the mouth before you accept it. Sometimes titles do not signify the role content.

Writing in *Management Week* (16 October 1991) after his spell at ICI, Sir John Harvey-Jones reflected on the pros and cons in this way:

I am very uncertain about whether the top job should really be two jobs or not. I have seen successful examples both of a combination of chairman and chief executive in the one, and an admittedly small number but nevertheless very successful examples of where a non-executive chairman has worked well and happily with a chief executive. There is no doubt that if the top job of chairman and principal executive officer are combined in one, the job is a killer. The outside, representational role is immensely time-consuming. The better known and more successful you are at projecting the image of your company, the more you are requested to do so.

There are real advantages to having the top job split between two people. It is easier to replace either one of them if some disaster happens, or if one or the other begins to be 'off the boil'. It is extremely difficult to replace a combined chairman and chief executive. You take a double risk for a start, and the actual mechanisms of replacement are difficult to effect. It is relatively easy to draw up the fields of responsibility of two people who share the top job. The non-executive job should be primarily directed to the management of the actual board, and the external environment, as well as ensuring that mechanisms are in place to develop strategies and clear policies on the many issues for which a board has responsibility. The other, the executive role, is then responsible for that process. The chairman is responsible for seeing that the board checks that their policies have been carried out by the chief executive.

The difficulty in such organizations is one of split responsibilities. An organization of this type calls for a degree of integration and understanding between the two top people which is often difficult to achieve. Moreover, it can fall into the trap which the Americans dislike so much, of a lack of clarity as to who is ultimately in charge, and where the buck actually stops.

While it does have some highly desirable characteristics of flexibility, it lacks some of the crispness of having the whole thing tied into one person. Certainly such an approach is an unpopular one in America, where again organizational theory seems to be rather starker than in the United Kingdom.

One advocate for the American model – an executive chairman or chairman of the board with full executive powers which he or she may share by delegation with another officer (formerly called a managing director or chief operating officer) was Hugh Parker, a former regional head of McKinsey. Writing in the *Director* (April 1990) he delineated their respective roles in the process of what he called 'corporate renewal', taking over Sir John Harvey-Jones's definition of it as 'creating tomorrow's company out of today's'.

It is the chairman's role to:

- Create and work with a board that is capable of helping and supporting him in the overall direction and governance of the enterprise.
- Create a strategic vision for the business that derives realistically from the company's existing strengths, and that builds on its distinctive competitive advantages.
- Establish the basic properties, ethical values, policies and attitudes within the company that will transform it from being a 'repeating' culture into a 'learning' culture.

- Set standards of performance in terms of such criteria as product quality, customer service, technological leadership, market share, and financial measures that will ensure an above-average p/e ratio.
- Appoint a managing director with a clear mandate to achieve established standards of operating and financial performance. Monitor the managing director's performance against these standards, help and support him. But if and when necessary, replace him.

It is the role of the managing director, together with his top management team, to:

- Ensure that operational planning and financial control systems are in place, appropriate to the new management organizational structures of each business unit.
- Ensure that operating objectives and standards of performance are not only understood but also 'owned' at all levels of the enterprise – i.e. are seen to be challenging, but realistic and attainable.
- Closely monitor operating and financial results of each business against agreed plans and budgets. Take remedial action where necessary.
- Develop business strategies and operating plans that reflect the longer-term corporate objectives and priorities established by the board. Maintain an ongoing conversation with the chairman and board to ensure that these objectives and priorities are constantly adjusted to reflect changes in the external environment.
- Restructure the business portfolio in line with the board's decisions that determine the future shape and strategy of the business. Redraw the management organization structure to reflect the restructured business.
- Undertake a programme for systematically strengthen-

ing management at all levels – but especially at the
higher levels – by training, retraining, development,
delegation, motivation, recruitment and replacement.

If you compare these two lists of functions with the seven
generic functions that compose the role of a strategic leader
(see page 85), you can see that what is happening here is
essentially the sharing of one role. There are not two arche-
typal roles, as it were, in the generic script – only one.

The point is that in an organizational situation where
there is a split role, everything depends upon the ability of
the two parties to work out a division of labour that makes
sense to them both. So numerous are the variables of
experience, temperament, tradition and personal chemistry
that there are no rules or principles, except that each should
be clear about what is expected and what they expect. The
resulting sub-roles are bound to overlap, and both parties
must be able to cope with some ambiguity and handle issues
where the shoe is pinching as they arise. If either the
chairman or the chief executive/managing director are lacking in sufficient practical wisdom, the relationship will end
up in divorce.

The essence of a successful 'job-sharing' relationship at
the top is that it should be a true partnership of minds and
spirits, but with complementary rather than identical
interests, abilities and temperaments. There should be mutu-
ality of trust and understanding between chairman and chief
executive, there should be a shared set of strategic objectives,
and above all there should be so much sharing of perceptions
and values that each can coordinate with the other, almost
without having to discuss an issue at all.

CHOOSING THE TOP TEAM

Few strategic leaders apart from democratically elected strategic leaders such as the US President and the British Prime Minister have the luxury of choosing their team from scratch. Most inherit a top team and can only make changes if they move people out or replace those who leave or retire. The latter can be a lengthy process, and it takes some strategic leaders years to achieve the team they want. Yet there are few more important things you can do than to choose the right people for the top jobs.

As a general observation, the most common weakness of strategic leaders is lack of judgement about people. It is rather like driving a car: we all think we are good at it, but how many of us really are? Believing that you can 'spot a winner' is as hazardous in organizations as it is on the racecourse. It is lack of judgement about people that leads to wrong choices in the first place or over-promotion. The deployment of carefully designed and led selection boards can compensate in part, but even so the strategic leader's influence tends to be decisive for or against. For the most senior appointments you should always be on the selection board – if not in the chair.

'Two minds are better than one' when it comes to judging the fitness of a person for a role – providing both minds are wise. For judgement about people is really just one aspect of *phronesis*. The best case studies I have come across of the process whereby a person with *phronesis* in this respect forms a judgement of another person in interactions over a course of time are the six novels of Jane Austen. There is a price to be paid in getting judgements of people wrong. If someone is not up to the mark and you have to find a replacement, think of the extra time and cost. Yes, you have learnt a lesson. It is a cheque paid into your experience bank. But think of the cost! 'Experience is the best of schoolmasters,' said Thomas Carlyle, 'only the school fees are heavy.' Get it right first time. Here are five tips for teambuilding, whether it be the board or the executive team that directly reports to you, gleaned from my own experience:

- Avoid selecting clones of yourself. You are looking for a balanced team, with complementary mental gifts of intelligence and imagination, technical and professional experience and interests relevant to your field.
- Always choose a person of real ability and stature, not those who can be guaranteed to accept the party line, agree with what you say and never challenge you in debate before decisions. If you appoint 'safe' people who will do your bidding without a word, you are only advertising your own weakness and insecurity.
- You are taking on a whole person, and great strengths are usually accompanied by great weaknesses. A wise and mature team can accommodate far more idiosyncrasies in the best people – providing they *are* the best – than a fragile one.
- Never write off a new team member too quickly. A person of ability may have been placed – by you or your predecessor – in the wrong role. Reassigned to another, that person may grow wings and fly.
- The opinion of the team on a prospective new member is always worth seeking. But remember that new appointments are ways of changing and improving the team, lifting it out of its comfort zone. Don't expect the team to see the pearl when you present them with someone who looks like grit.

The sign of a great strategic leader, one who is both excellent in leadership and credited with unassailable professional reputation, is his or her ability to lead highly complex and often over-confident individuals. Who, one might ask, would be able to hold together brilliant but wayward contributors such as Montgomery and Patton in the same top team? Yet Alexander and Eisenhower both achieved that difficult feat. It is significant, as I said earlier, that both these Supreme Commanders were men of genuine humility.

CASE STUDY: LINCOLN AND STANTON

Edwin M. Stanton first met the future President Abraham Lincoln in 1855 when both men, as attorneys, were involved in the same court case. Stanton, renowned as a lawyer, evidently insulted the less well-known Lincoln, allegedly calling him a giraffe. He was equally critical of Lincoln during his rise to power, talking dismissively of him as a man with 'no token of any intelligent understanding'.

Yet despite this negative attitude towards him personally, Lincoln made Stanton the new Secretary of War in his Cabinet team, for he knew him to be the best man for the role. Stanton took on the challenge with enthusiasm and set about fully justifying his selection. Within a few months he reorganized the War Department and led it into becoming a much more effective body. Tireless in his efforts, he worked all hours of the day to merit the trust that Lincoln had placed in him.

Stanton soon revised his early opinion of Lincoln, while the President for his part appreciated more and more the reliable administrative abilities of the Secretary of War, and the solid worth of the man as opposed to his somewhat surly appearance and manner. As their mutual trust grew, Lincoln was able to delegate most completely to him. On 9 April 1865, on Lincoln's return to Washington, it was Stanton who greeted him with a warm embrace and the news that Lee had surrendered at Appomattox. And no man wept more when Lincoln was assassinated than Stanton.

CHALLENGES TO TEAMWORK

Whether you are leading a board of directors or its equivalent (such as a cabinet or council of governors) or a senior executive team of operational leaders and staff specialists, you should expect to deal with the complexity that arises from the tendency of senior and really able people to be complex. Gifted but complex individuals are usually highly idiosyncratic: they evolve their own ways of doing things and need to be broken in gently, like wild mustangs, to the necessity of teamwork.

With all individual team members – and you as their leader are no exception – there is always a balance between their actual or potential contribution to the task and their eccentricity – some characteristic, action, practice or habit that differs in some way from what is usual or expected. An eccentric individual presents a strangeness or irregularity that may be harmless, but that is an ingrained part of the personality. Idiosyncrasy also suggests a strangeness of nature but less a divergence from the general (with a suggestion sometimes of at least mild mental aberration) evidence of a strongly independent personality – the following of one's own bent or temperament with strong individuality and independence of action.

A mature team will always live with idiosyncrasy and reasonable eccentricity (if there is such a thing!), providing the gift or talent is there. It would have been most unwise of a commander-in-chief to dismiss Nelson before Trafalgar because he flaunted social custom and propriety by living openly with his mistress. Not that his sailors would have cared tuppence.

In all teams, experience suggests, there are potential 'team maintenance' cracks, fissures as invisible as metal fatigue cracks on the wing of an aircraft that will give way under pressure. It may be a matter of interpersonal chemistry – X does not get on well with Y. Under normal circumstances all is well, but if things go badly X will tend to blame Y, and vice versa. They fall into the kind of conflict that Milton described so well in *Paradise Lost*:

> Thus they the fruitless hours
> In mutual accusation spent
> Neither self-condemning.

Or there could be a potential division – a hairline crack – along the lines of gender or ethnic background or profession. In some companies that are struggling, for example, you may find that sales and marketing blame production and vice versa, or there is a civil war between the accountants and the rest. Nor have all traces disappeared of that deeply ingrained divide between 'management' and 'work people', especially where the latter are strongly unionized.

Don't imagine that because you have reached the top of an organization you have passed beyond 'team maintenance' problems. If you lead the board in the context of the British business system or similar ones, for example, you will have a potential crack on your plate between executive and non-executive directors (in Japan the latter do not exist). As a business strategic leader with board responsibility in such a context you will need to think out carefully the qualities and abilities you are looking for in *both* kinds of director. Non-executive directors should have *phronesis* that commands respect from their executive colleagues, and if they have that they will acquire what knowledge they need of the actual business to perform their role as informed but independent and wise counsel.

Teamwork in the boardroom is essential, not least because it sends a positive message throughout the organization. 'Example is not the main thing in influencing others – it is the only thing,' said Albert Schweitzer. It has immense practical value, too, in that it affects the speed and quality of decisions.

Sir John Harvey-Jones, a former Royal Navy Officer, believed firmly that a board of directors should be like Nelson's band of brothers:

> The speed at which a company can move depends, to a large extent, on the speed at which the board itself can move, for, while boards can seldom create the opportunities which exist for businesses further down the line, they have demonstrated over and over again their ability to stop such opportunities being seized or developed. My ideal board is an enabling board, which adds value to the effort of people below and enables everyone, from the top to the bottom of the company, to give of his best. *To achieve this it is really essential that the board itself should be a team.* It is impossible to act as an enabling mechanism if there are unresolved fundamental differences between parts the group which shares the responsibility for the direction of the company.

PROBLEMS WITH TOP LEADERSHIP TEAMS

Strategic leadership of an enterprise is a shared activity. To be successful you need a capable and effective top leadership team – your senior operational or executive leaders, including heads of staff functions such as finance. These teams characteristically range in size from five to fourteen, and that sort of span does not have any correlation with the size of an organization. There are five main types of problem that arise in top teams.

Problem 1: Inadequate capabilities of an individual operational leader

Sometimes an operational leader will fail to grasp the strategic implications, such as when they deliver short-term profits by using short-sighted means that are detrimental to the values and longer-term interests that you are working for. Or you may have concerns about their style, such as lack of personal time management or failing to do what they said they would do, or lack of a sense of urgency. Arrogance or overt ambition may constitute other causes for concern.

Often the problematic person is more of a manager – competent in running the day-to-day business and an adequate staff administrator – than a leader. He or she lacks a strategic perspective and personal leadership and team-working skills. Such a person can manage a business but cannot *grow* the business. Counselling and coaching seldom do much good. Either you or your predecessor made an error in selection, and you should consider replacing the inadequate operational leader. It is never a mistake to turn back if you are on the wrong road. As a strategic leader you are paid to face unpleasant situations and make tough decisions such as sacking colleagues. Too often chief executives press ahead despite problems with individuals instead of confronting embarrassing or awkward issues and dealing with them at board level. In Japan this evasion reaches an art form!

Problem 2: Common team-wide shortcomings

As a new strategic leader you may come to the conclusion sooner or later that your top team as a whole – usually with one or two exceptions – is not up to either the challenges of its new competitive environment or the complexity and magnitude of the organization they are supposed to be leading. Swift growth, geographical expansion and diversification tend to breed this mismatch between today's opportunities and a top team that belongs to yesterday. Bringing the capabilities of the top team into balance with present realities and future aspirations is a complex challenge for any strategic leader, however experienced.

Problem 3: Harmful rivalries

These usually manifest as a particular rivalry between two individuals. They tend to start out as disagreements, often legitimate, over some aspect of the common business, before they blossom into full-blown feuds complete with personal abuse. Before you as the leader realize how serious it is, personal acrimony has flared out of control like a fire and threatens ever more serious consequences. Even after you or someone else – perhaps a wise non-executive director – have attempted to mediate, the issue may not so much go away as go to ground. At least if the rivalry is submerged it can do less damage.

Harmful rivalries of this politico-personal nature are symptoms of lack of team spirit and they should never happen. A friendly rivalry between parts of the whole is natural and, within reason, to be encouraged; there is a tension between certain individuals that can be positive rather than negative. But a good leader today is 100 per cent in the role of a leader (the three circles), 100 per cent in the role of colleague and

100 per cent in the role of subordinate. Nelson achieved full marks in all three roles, and so you must expect something more than pass marks for your top team.

Problem 4: Groupthink

Unexamined and unconscious assumptions, too easy agreement, a low tolerance for any conflicting debate about ideas, an unwillingness to confront, an implicit belief that what is unanimous must be right – these are some of the symptoms of groupthink. Superficially a team affected with this disease may appear healthy to an observer, in that its discussions are amicable, smooth-running and harmonious, often punctuated by much laughter. But look at the quality of its decisions, for 'by their fruits you shall know them'.

Cohesiveness in your top team, and a degree of like-mindedness in terms of purpose and values, is essential. But you should make it clear that you expect people to voice the truth as they see it. You and others may not agree but this is a secondary matter. To put group cohesion – in mind – over and above the task, which in the case of the board or senior executive group is to make the best decision, is to invert the three circle model and to court disaster.

The necessity for disagreement

Unless one has considered alternatives, one has a closed mind.

This, above all, explains why effective decision-makers deliberately disregard the second major command of the textbooks on decision-making and create dissension and disagreement, rather than consensus.

Decisions of the kind the executive has to make are not made well by acclamation. They are made well only if based on the clash of conflicting views, with dialogue between different points of view, the choice between different judge-ments. The first rule in decision-making is that one does not make a decision unless there is disagreement.

Alfred P. Sloan is reported to have said at a meeting of one of his top committees: 'Gentlemen, I take it we are all in complete agreement on the decision here.' Everyone around the table nodded assent. 'Then,' continued Mr Sloan, 'I pro-pose we postpone further discussion of this matter until our next meeting to give ourselves time to develop disagreement and perhaps gain some understanding of what the decision is all about.'

Sloan was anything but an 'intuitive' decision-maker. He always emphasized the need to test opinions against facts and the need to make absolutely sure that one did not start out with the conclusion and then look for the facts that would support it. But he knew that the right decision demands adequate disagreement.

Peter Drucker, *The Effective Executive* (1967)

Problem 5: Fragmentation

Some top teams are in name only – part of the rhetoric that second-rate chairmen and chief executives pick up and use but don't have written on their hearts. A group of individuals is not a team. Even if they meet together from time to time, operational leaders in charge of relatively independent spheres will not feel part of a team unless they view and share the common purpose of the whole enterprise, perceive themselves as stakeholders in that vision, and can see that their part – however important and relatively autonomous – is complementary to other parts in the organization.

Symptoms of fragmentation include lack of cooperation between the parts, failure to share information, decision making regardless of the broad strategic direction, meetings of the top 'team' that are perfunctory and marred by absenteeism, the growth of separate agendas, and a particularism – exclusive or special devotion to a particular interest – that informs the thinking and action of each of the individuals in the team. The only person concerned or caring about the whole as opposed to the parts is *you*. If you are interested in having heart attacks, remember this simple equation: Fragmentalization = Hospitalization.

Of course, strategic leadership works in the opposite direction. The chief issue in all organizations is getting the balance of the parts and the whole right. The operational leader should be *both* head of a part *and* a member of the strategic leadership team that under your direction is responsible for the whole. All that fragmentation at the top reveals is that you have failed to fulfil one essential function in your role as a strategic leader.

CASE STUDY: HOW TO WIN TOP TEAM COMMITMENT

Horatio Nelson was born on 29 September 1758 at Burnham Thorpe in Norfolk. Forty years later he destroyed Napoleon's fleet at the Battle of the Nile and turned the Great War with France in Britain's favour. Then, in 1805, he led a fleet that he had kept in fighting trim at sea for two years, mainly from its own resources, 3,000 miles across the Atlantic and back again. Finally, his victory at Trafalgar raised the reputation of the Royal Navy to such a height that it was not challenged again for over a hundred years, and laid the foundations of the British Empire.

Nelson's lifelong friend Collingwood wrote of him: 'He possessed the zeal of an enthusiast, directed by talents which nature had very boastfully bestowed on him, and everything seemed, as if by enchantment, to prosper under his direction. But it was the effect of system, and nice calculation, not of chance.'

It was in the art of leading men in war that Nelson's genius shone most brightly. In command of the inshore squadron at Cadiz and in the gallant failure of Tenerife he had shown courage, energy and readiness to risk not only his life but his reputation for the sake of getting at the enemy – a good example and a source of confidence to his followers. But there was more than this. Hitherto Nelson had commanded detachments; in the campaign that ended in the victory of the Nile he was in sole command.

'It was his practice during the whole of his cruise,' wrote Berry, his fleet captain, 'whenever the weather and circumstances would permit, to have his captains on board the *Vanguard*, where he would fully develop to them his own ideas of the different and best modes of attack, in all possible positions.' In eight weeks he had made of them a band of brothers. Admiral Lord Hone said of the victory to Berry: 'It stood unparalleled and singular in this instance, that every captain distinguished himself.'

In other words, Nelson gave only the simplest directions to his captains, relying on the intelligent responses of his 'band of brothers' as they faced particular opportunities. And it worked. For example, at the Nile it was Captain Foley of the *Goliath* who saw that the shoal water between the anchored line of French ships and the shore was just deep enough to allow a British attack on the unprepared landward quarter. As the US Admiral Mahan put it, 'It is in entire keeping with Nelson's well-known character, that, after discussing all likely positions and ascertaining that his captains understood his views, he should with perfect and generous confidence have left all the details of the immediate action with them.' His book, *The Influence of Sea Power upon the*

French Revolution and Empire carried Nelson's leadership style to generations of later natural strategic leaders.

Although you could say that Nelson's discussions with his captains centred more on tactics than strategy, the principle holds good. You need to share your strategic overview and strategic ideas with your operational leaders, leaving them free to plan and act in an opportunity-centred, entrepreneurial way. By entrepreneurial here I mean someone who bears the risk of success or failure, profit or loss.

As a strategic leader you can reduce the risks by holding the kind of discussions with your top team that Nelson conducted informally around the dinner table in his cabin. By revealing your thinking in that way you will convey to operational leaders what decisions you expect them to make themselves and what decisions they should naturally discuss first with you. The latter will obviously include, for example, any course of action where the downside of the risk – the consequences of failure – could hole your enterprise below the waterline.

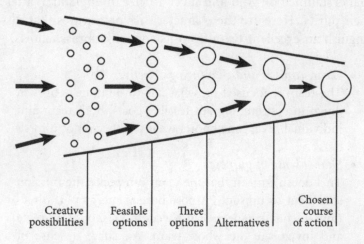

| Creative possibilities | Feasible options | Three options | Alternatives | Chosen course of action |

The lobster pot model of decision making

The journey ahead will then be an adventure. Moreover, when you have freed your top team from the fear of failure you will have opened their eyes to all possibilities. And when they see possibilities in abundance, then they can make better decisions. The following mode highlights the part played in creative possibilities, visible only to those who are unafraid to consider them in the decision-making process.

THE HALLMARKS OF TEAM EXCELLENCE

How can you improve your powers as teambuilder, given the complexities, potential problems and challenges outlined earlier? The answer is simple: form a clear concept in your mind of what an excellent team looks like. Then, like an automatic pilot, this concept will serve to guide you in all that you do and say to achieve it.

Hallmarks (from Goldsmiths' Hall in London, where gold and silver articles were assayed and stamped) are official marks stamped on gold and silver articles in England to attest their purity. Here are the characteristics or features that distinguish an excellent team from its copper or brass fellows:

- *Clear, realistic and challenging objectives*
  The team is focused on what has to be done – broken down into stretching but feasible goals, both team and individual. Everyone knows what is expected of him or her.
- *Shared sense of purpose*
  This doesn't mean that the team can recite the mission statement in unison! Purpose here is energy plus direction – what engineers call a vector. It should animate and invigorate the whole team. All share a sense of ownership and responsibility for team success.

- *Best use of resources*
  A high-performance team means that resources are allocated for strategic reasons for the good of the whole. They are not seen as the private property of any part of the organization. Resources include people and their time, not just money and material.

- *Progress review*
  The willingness to monitor its own progress and to generate improvements characterize excellent teams. These improvements encompass process – *how* we work together – as well as tasks – *what* we do together.

- *Building on experience*
  A blame culture mars any team. Errors will be made, but the greatest error of all is to do nothing so as to avoid making any! A wise team learns from failure, realizing that success teaches us nothing and continual success may breed arrogance.

- *Mutual trust and support*
  A good team trusts its members to pursue their part in the common task. Appreciation is expressed and recognition given. People play to each other's strengths and cover each other's weaknesses. The level of mutual support is high. The atmosphere is one of openness and trust.

- *Communication*
  People listen to one another and build on one another's contributions. They communicate openly, freely and with skill (clear, concise, simple and with tact). Issues, problems and weaknesses are not sidestepped. Differences of opinion are respected. Team members know when to be very supportive and sensitive, and when to challenge and be intellectually tough.

- *Riding out the storms*
  In times of turbulent change it is never going to be all plain sailing. When unavoidable storms and crises arise,

an excellent team rises to the challenge and demonstrates its sterling worth. It has resilience.

Where these eight hallmarks – in no order of importance –
are present, people enjoy working together as a team more
deeply. They have fun, like other teams, but so rare is the
experience of working in an excellent team that the enjoyment and fun are transformed by hindsight into the true
gold and silver of enduring satisfaction and a sense of
gratitude.

KEY POINTS: BUILDING THE TOP TEAM

- Who is your top team? That depends upon your own
  allotted role. You may be a leader of the board or council
  (the strategy- and policy-making body) and leader of the
  executive team. Or the role of strategic leader may be split
  into two.
- This is nothing new – Sparta always had two kings and
  republican Rome two consuls. It helps with the workload
  and provides a check against abuse of power. On the other
  hand, a single strategic leader enjoys the advantages of
  'unity of command', especially useful in times of crisis.
- In split-role situations it is vitally important to establish a
  truly complementary and harmonious working partnership, so that the expectations of both persons and their
  respective sub-roles are as clear as possible. There will be
  overlaps, so constant communication is necessary.
- Organizations take their drumbeat from the top. If the
  board of directors (or its equivalent) works as a team,
  then you have more than half solved the problem of
  getting the whole organization to see itself as one great
  team and to act like one.

- One of your major challenges as a strategic leader is to ensure that the calibre and capability of your top executive team match the complexity of its environment, the turbulent seas through which it must navigate the ship.
- Whatever its shape or composition, *your* team at the top should have the following hallmarks:

  - Clear, realistic and challenging objectives
  - Shared sense of purpose
  - Best use of resources
  - Progress review

  - Building on experience
  - Mutual trust and support
  - Communication
  - Riding out the storms

How do you know you have won? When the energy is coming the other way and when your people are visibly growing individually and as a group.

Sir John Harvey-Jones, former Chairman of ICI and TV business guru

7

GETTING THE
STRATEGY RIGHT

'All men can see the tactics whereby I conquer,
but what none can see is the strategy out of which
victory is evolved.'

Sun Tzu (fourth century B. C.)

As a strategic leader your prime responsibility is to ensure
that your organization is going in the right direction. That
sounds simple enough but it is not always easy to achieve.
What *is* the right strategic direction? How or where do you
establish it? Why is implementation so difficult?

We can break the problem into two parts: identifying the
best strategy and pursuing it to the desired result. Although
these two parts in reality are interwoven, it makes sense to
separate out the *thinking* side of it. That is what I call
strategic thinking.

It is useful, I think, to distinguish between such *strategic
thinking* on the one hand and *strategic planning* on the
other. Strategic thinking is thinking about the longer term
and the more important ends in any situation – including
your own life – and the pathways that may or may not
lead to them. If and when you can identify such an end or

set of ends, and choose among the possible pathways the ones that make most sense, the process of corporate planning can get under way. It is daft to launch into a strategic planning exercise before your strategic thought has come to some working conclusions, although, believe me, this does happen.

It is not possible to teach anyone to think strategically if they cannot do it, for strategic thinking is a function of *phronesis*, practical wisdom, which is neither an art nor a science nor a skill. Therefore this chapter will be short! All that I can do is to remove some common misconceptions about strategic thinking. I must be honest and admit that there are misconceptions I have harboured myself, and only my customary struggle to be clear has revealed to me my own hidden assumptions. Not that I am entirely clear even now, but let me share with you what I have learned so far. These are all things that have helped me to become a better strategic thinker.

'But you said just now that strategic thinking is something that you either can do or you can't.'

You shouldn't believe everything I say. Perhaps I meant that it cannot be *taught*, but you can certainly *learn* to do it better. Remember that *phronesis* includes the capacity to learn, not least through experience.

THE INVENTION OF STRATEGY

It helps me to remember that strategy really doesn't exist! To remind you, *strategy* in ancient Greek meant the whole art of a commander-in-chief, including leadership, administration and working with allies, as well as knowing how to bring an enemy to battle and what tactics to employ. Strategy, if you like, was the thinking of a *strategos*, a general, and he had a lot to think about apart from the conduct of military operations. As armies became larger and warfare more complex, strategy was introduced as a new concept in contrast to tactics. But strategy was still about what a general thought it best to do in order to achieve victory. It was not something that existed, so to speak, separately, that you could read in a book or learn on a course.

That began to change when General Henri Jomini wrote a book on the principles that guided Napoleon in his strategic thinking and his art of generalship, an art for which he claimed, not entirely modestly, that he had genius. Napoleon read the book with some alarm – 'It teaches my whole system of war to my enemies,' he muttered to a friend. Then he quickly regained his composure, saying with a smile: 'The old generals who command against me will never read it, and the young men who read it do not command!'

The study by Henri Jomini and Carl von Clausewitz of how Napoleon's mind worked gave rise to the Principles of War (an essay by Clausewitz that later expanded into the book *On War*, which covers the whole art of generalship), including some strategic ideas such as that of concentrating decisive force at the critical point – though Alexander the Great, Hannibal or Caesar could also have thought up that one. But there was no strategy. Captain Sir Basil Liddell-Hart, who called himself a military strategist, claimed that he had discovered the strategy of the indirect approach. General Archibald Wavell pointed out to him that he could have written an equally weighted book on the strategy of the direct approach! Direct or indirect, it all depends on the situation. We don't think any the worse of Montgomery as a general because he made a direct frontal assault at Alamein, for he had no alternative.

If you cannot find a thing called strategy in the military field, the source of the term, what were the first business writers actually borrowing? If you look at their books you will find a muddled understanding.

The first of these was William Newman's *Administrative Action: The techniques of Organization and Management* (1951). Remarking that 'the matter of strategy' is little discussed, he defined its usage in his book as 'the adjustment of a plan to the anticipated reaction of those who will be affected by the plan'. You don't get more muddled than that.

The first serious writer on business strategy was Alfred Chandler. His *Chapters in the History of American Enterprise* (1962) began as a study of how large corporations had responded to the new environment of post-war expansion in the US. He focused on nine companies who had innovated with new organizational designs, some dating back to the 1920s, and then on four of them – General Motors, DuPont, Standard Oil of New Jersey and Sears, Roebuck. Organizational structure, he argued, had been changed fittingly as new business strategies were adopted.

These giant corporations were like armies, and their corporate headquarters (a military term) housed general staff. Chandler advocated that there should be an 'administrator' at the top of the 'general office' to oversee strategic planning, which he defined as 'the determination of the basic long-term goals and objectives of an enterprise, and the adoption of courses of action and the allocation of resources necessary for carrying out these goals'. Chandler accepted that strategic planning could happen at various levels in the organizational hierarchy, but he reserved the prerogative of resource allocation to the 'general office' at the top. This general office, composed of 'general executives' and staff specialists, existed to 'coordinate, appraise and plan goals and policies and allocate resources for quasi-autonomous divisions' in order to meet short-term and long-term fluctuations and developments in the market. It is not hard to see here a reflection of the modern military model of strategic planning – as exemplified by the German general staff in both World Wars, but common to all armies. The Pentagon is the symbol of this model.

Mesmerized by the military model of *strategic planning*, the early business writers gave little or no attention to the process of *strategic thinking*. Strategic planning was a corporate product, the new output of head office, which largely justified the large general staff – Shell even called its executive restaurants 'messes' and they were graded by the rank of those who could use them. Meanwhile, in Russia, even vaster bureaucracies in the head offices of ministries and departments in Moscow were producing Twenty-, Ten- and Five-Year plans regulating the goals and objectives of an entire economy. This orthodox view of strategic planning, alias corporate strategy, was set out in an influential book by Professor Kenneth Andrews of Harvard Business School, entitled *The Concept of Corporate Strategy* (1971):

> Corporate strategy is the pattern of decisions in a company that determines and reveals its objectives, purposes, or goals, produces the principal policies and plans for achieving those goals, and defines the range of business the company is to pursue, the kind of economic and human organization it is or intends to be, and the nature of the economic and non-economic contribution it intends to make to its shareholders, employees, customers and communities.

The 'pattern of decisions' essentially means a plan. But Andrews did make an important contribution to understanding and improving the process of strategic thinking that precedes any form of planning. He advocated what became known as a SWOT analysis – that organizations should appraise carefully their Strengths, Weaknesses, Opportunities and Threats as a prelude to corporate strategy. He also stressed the importance of scanning the changing environment, using the ready-made headings of Political, Economic, Social and Technological (PEST) to consider the salient factors. These are now called 'tools' and are often no more than mental drills, substitutes for thinking rather than signposts for it. Eventually, in the field of business, the discussion of strategy has become dominated by the concept of *marketing* – the action, business or process of promoting and selling goods or services, including market research, choice of product, pricing and quality, advertising and distribution. A business strategic leader today is not short of advice – if he or she is prepared to pay for it – on what 'strategy' to adopt. The increased complexity of markets – now for most businesses a global one – has created another market for management consultants and business school gurus. The latter often sell strategic ideas, which prove to be simplistic – like Dionysodorus (see page 8), they do not tell you how to adapt their 'strategies' to your unique circumstances; nor can you claim your money back if their nostrums don't work. The former – the management consultants – will even offer to do your strategic thinking for you, but is it all that difficult?

UNFREEZING YOUR STRATEGIC THINKING

The concept of a strategic leader takes us back to the origins of *strategia*, the art of being a leader-in-chief. Strategy is simply the thinking appropriate to someone at that level of leadership responsibility, and it embraces far more than military operations or marketing strategy. It is the product of an individual mind, not the output of a corporate staff at head office. So you do need to know how to think strategically, as distinct from the organizational process of setting goals and objectives, allocating resources and coordinating activities – a higher level of *planning*.

Divorcing strategic thinking from strategic planning is the first step to loosening up your mind. The next step is to rid yourself from the permafrost belief that strategy is somehow very difficult and complex, quite beyond your powers even if you could credit yourself with an average level of common sense or *phronesis*. In fact the *environment* in which you work as a strategic leader *is* complex, both for general reasons and reasons to do with our own time and age. But strategic thinking is always simple. The complexity lies more in execution than conception.

Some people seem to have strategic sense while others lack it. You can actually develop your strategic sense by reflecting on the adjective *strategic*. Why do we call something *strategic*? At the most general level it has two elements:

Importance	To be able to distinguish between the important, the less important and the unimportant, is the starting-point. If it is important it is marked by or possesses weight or consequence. It has evident value, either generally or in particular relation, and often by merely existing.
Longer term	How long is long? That all depends. But *strategic* implies a longer-term perspective rather than the short-term view. Indeed, to think strategically may mean trading short-term gain for long-term advantage.

People in any field who possess *phronesis* – intelligence, experience and goodness – tend to develop a strategic sense in general terms. In other words, by thought and experience, they evolve a *philosophy*, a mental framework of strategic ideas, which serves as the foundation for their strategic thinking in any aspect of their work. This philosophy is essentially the answer to the double question: What is really important for success in this field? What produces value in the longer term?

EXERCISE 1: Take five principles
Take some paper and write down the five principles or essentials that anyone in your field has to get right if they are going to lead an organization within it to success.

ENDS AND MEANS

Strategy is customarily defined along the lines of the art or skill of carefully planning towards a goal. A simpler way of understanding strategic thinking is to see it as a form of ends-means thinking.

There are several basic relations in thinking. One is the relation of *cause* and *effect*, which is central, for example, in scientific thinking. The relation between the two terms is not arbitrary, for at all times and in all places *cause* must precede *effect*. That is why you can never be born before your own mother.

The relation between *means* and *ends* is a similar basic distinction. Strategic thinking is about relating means to ends, but the ends in question – be they organizational or individual – are *important* and *longer-term*. You may be considering how to cook your meat and vegetables (means) for a dinner-party (end) tonight, but you are not thinking strategically.

You can see why so much ink has been spilt in advising strategic leaders to be clear about the *end*, variously called vision, mission, purpose, aim, goal or objective. The first Principle of War, you may recall, is Selection of Maintenance of the Aim. But what is the aim? What constitutes *means* and what *ends*? This is not always easy to determine, for what is an *end* at one level of thought is a *means* upon the next level up. Take the military as an example.

Ask most generals engaged in a war what the *end* is and they will reply in a word, 'Victory'. Understandably, for if you are in a competitive situation where one must either win or lose, obviously winning is the immediate end. Many a chief executive in business would echo the thought. 'We are in a fiercely competitive market,' they would say. 'Our goal is to be the winner or one of the winners, and not to find ourselves the losers who go out of business.' As we have seen, business strategy theory focuses entirely on that end.

It was Carl von Clausewitz, a former Prussian officer with a philosophical mind, who left his mark in the voluminous and turgid *On War* with one simple and seminal principle. War, he declared, is always a *means* to a political *end*; in his famous phrase, it is 'politics carried on by other means'.

This relation of military strategy (ends and means) to the political level above it, so that military operations had significance only as means to a potential end or aim, had a profound influence on the military. As I discussed in Chapter 4, it meant that *strategia* as the art of a commander-in-chief now had to encompass the ability to work well with the 'political' master. Military commanders at all levels also needed to understand the political rationale of a military operation, or why they were being asked to carry it out.

The profound influence of Clausewitz's perception of *end* and *means* in war is reflected in this definition of strategic thinking and planning by Field Marshal Viscount

Alanbrooke, who served as the head of the British Army, Churchill's chief-of-staff and his principal military adviser for most of the Second World War. The objects of strategy are:

> ... to determine the aim, which should be political: to derive from that aim a series of military objectives to be achieved: to assess these objectives as to the military requirements they create, and the pre-conditions which the achievement of each is likely to necessitate: to measure available and potential resources against the requirements and to chart from this process a coherent pattern of priorities and a rational course of action.

In *The Art of Judgment* (1969), Sir Geoffrey Vickers made the seminal point that all the ends we pursue can be expressed in terms of changes in relation. To defeat an enemy, for example, if you happened to be a Roman general, meant that the vanquished entered into a new relation with you – slavery. The wealth and land you plundered and conquered gave you wealth, which changed your relation with others in a thousand direct or subtle ways. Or at least you might hope it would do so. Fame also changed your relative position in the list of those competing for high office in Rome.

The end of international diplomacy is for better relations between nations and to mutual benefit. If the relation we call peace – however troubled and uneasy it may be – is lost, then the political end is to restore it as a step towards a better place, a better relation with that temporary enemy.

War is, of course, a very imperfect means towards that end of a 'better peace', though in some circumstances it is a necessary evil in so far as it is the least worst option. For the nature of war is to arouse even deeper hostility, to exacerbate the latent aggression in all of us, and sow the seeds of hatred for generations to come. Clausewitz pointed out that the *means* politicians adopted when they went to war had its own inherent logic, and might well impose on them requirements or conditions that lay counter to the ultimate political end. This 'kick-back' factor is more significant in a nuclear age, which has had some impact on the potential for conventional large-scale wars between nations, certainly on a worldwide scale like that of the Second World War.

THE CASE OF SIR WILLIAM WALLER

Most murders are family affairs, and civil wars can be murderous affairs. Yet one general in the English Civil War (1642–46) who always kept in mind the vision of a 'better peace' was Sir William Waller, subject of a biography by me entitled *Roundhead General* (1997).

Waller was an active, bold and valiant general who commanded Parliament's army in the west of England and then in the south, vigorously fighting battles, engaging in skirmishes and taking towns by siege. When his old and close friend Ralph Hopton, a Royalist general of the opposing army, wrote to suggest a meeting, Waller tactfully declined by letter adding:

> That great God, which is the searcher of my heart, knows with what a sad sense I go upon this service, and with what a perfect hatred I detest *this war without an enemy* . . . We are both upon the stage and must act those parts assigned us in this tragedy. Let us do it in the way of honour, and without personal animosities.

Waller won the ensuing battle. One Royalist prisoner, a young lieutenant, was captured unhurt, but was cruelly shot twice by a Scottish professional soldier. When he saw him Waller was exceedingly angry, sent for his own doctor immediately and did not leave the man until his wounds had been dressed. Waller also paid an innkeeper for the lieutenant's lodging, allowed him to send for a woman to care for him, and lastly gave him ten silver shillings for his personal expenses.

Waller would not have needed Clausewitz to tell him that the aim of the Civil War was political rather than military. He was a Member of Parliament and ranked among its political leaders. Although (with Hopton) he had had some military experience when young, he had none of the assumptions of professional soldiers.

Waller always fought in the knowledge that one day Englishmen would need to live together again in harmony and peace, and – clear strategic thinker that he was – he avoided anything that would deepen rather than heal the division. He endured three years of imprisonment when Cromwell became military dictator. Upon his release, he worked secretly for a restoration of the old constitutional order that Charles I had destroyed through his deficiencies in practical wisdom. Waller lived to see a time once more 'when gardens only had their towers, and all the garrisons were flowers.'

The case study of Sir William Waller illustrates the importance of keeping the end of one's endeavours constantly in mind. In that context, the way Waller treated the maliciously wounded young lieutenant was not merely humane, it was *strategically* significant. For it was but one example of one of the *means* Waller deliberately adopted – a policy of being considerate and kind to prisoners – that contributed directly or indirectly towards his *end*, in the restoration of a true peace.

The first principle in strategic thinking, then, is to address the ends of your activities. What is the desired result? As specifically as possible, what do you have to achieve?

THE PRINCIPLE OF THINKING ONE LEVEL UP

Paradoxically, you will not understand your *end* until you see it as a *means* to another higher end. Therefore always think one level up.

You can always find that next level up by answering the question *why*. There are basically two ways of answering the question. One is related to *cause-and-effect*. '*Why* am I writing this book? *Because* someone asked me to do so a year ago.' Present activity is explained by something that happened in the past.

The other route belongs to the realm and *ends-and-means*. '*Why* am I writing this book? *In order to* help you, my reader, to be more effective as a strategic leader.' Here the orientation is to the future. For me, as I pen this page, the moment when you will read it is at least two years away.

> **EXERCISE 2: In order to . . .**
> Identify and write down one target you have set for yourself in the next twelve months. Beneath it complete this sentence: I hope to complete this objective *in order to . . .*

The more times you ask the *why* question in the context of *ends-and-means*, the higher you will go and the more general or abstract your answers will become. At a certain point – sooner rather than later! – you will cry 'halt!'. Unless, that is, your vocation is to be a philosopher. For we accept a lot of things as *ends-in-themselves*. They are striving for their own sake, and trying to see them as means to something else does not add to your understanding. The walk you take in the day is a means to the end of fitness or health, but there is little point in going on to ask *why* health? We all accept this as an *end-in-itself*, or, if you like, it has the self-evident end-value we call good.

Therefore where you choose to 'stick' in exploring the Chinese boxes of *ends* is where it seems natural for you to do so. For a general, for example, the political end he is given may be as far up the ladder he goes – for the military is a practical profession. Subject, of course, to the political end being a lawful and ethically defensible one, for the defence 'I was only obeying orders' is defective at any level of leadership responsibility.

What is the *end* a business strategy leader should have in mind? At one level it is clear enough, the business is manifestly the activity of producing and selling goods and services – now collectively called the product – at a profit. In a capitalistic economy, if you don't make a profit you tend to go out of business sooner or later. In a free society business is left with as much autonomy as possible to press on with this end, subject only to legalization to protect employees, investors, consumers and the environment – all part of the complexity which surrounds the strategic leader in business.

Although one school of thought tends to emphasize profits in the equation, while another school emphasizes the value of the produce, both are strategically important for a business leader. The *end* that lies on the next level up – above the production and marketing of product at profit – is the *wealth of nations*, which is a key constituent – but not the only one – in a yet more abstract concept of a *better global society*.

THE END OF BUSINESS

When Alfred P. Sloan, one of the prime architects of modern capitalism, published his autobiography, *My Years with General Motors* (1963), he gave a classic definition of the profit motive and the way it works.

'We presumed,' he wrote, 'that the first purpose in making a capital investment is the establishment of a business that will pay satisfactory dividends and preserve and increase its capital value. The primary object of the corporation, therefore, we declared, was to make money not just motor cars.'

The end of business, then, is to make money. But Sloan is talking about business here on one level of thought, like a general stating that the end of his military operations is victory. Yet, as Peter Drucker, who knew him well, told me in conversation:

> Sloan had limitations. He lived entirely within the corporation. He had tunnel vision. In *My Years with General Motors* Sloan has hardly any references to politics and none to the New Deal, the dominant social policy of the time. He had no concept of the relation of business and society. Born in 1876, he was essentially a nineteenth-century man. At work, totally aloof, yet a warm family man who loved his children. He was very keen on safety at work. A personally generous man, too, one who gave all his money away.

What Sloan lacked was the concept that, just as war (as Clausewitz was the first to articulate conceptually) is a means to a *political* end, so business is a means to a *social* end. To make business a means to a *political* end – communism, socialism or imperialism – is to court economic disaster, because business (like war) has its own inherent logic that has to be respected if it is to fulfil its social functions.

One business strategic leader who saw clearly the *social* end of business was Konosuke Matsushita. Born in 1894, the youngest of eight children, he belonged to a well-off farming family who lived near Osaka, Japan. After his father's disastrous speculation in the rice market impoverished the family, the nine-year old Konosuke was sent off to Osaka as a live-in apprentice, first to a bicycle dealer. He then joined Osaka Electric and was eventually promoted to inspector, but decided to go off on his own at the age of twenty-three. Together with his wife and brother-in-law he started his own company, Matsushita Electric, in 1918.

From these humble beginnings the company grew into an international corporation of more than 200,000 employees, guided by the acumen and charismatic leadership of Konosuke Matsushita, first as President, then as Chairman of the Board, and finally as Executive Adviser. He died in 1989 at the age of ninety-four.

Because Matsushita's management philosophy was firmly rooted in his concern for people and his own experiences, his philosophy has had much influence in Japan; it particularly appealed to those in small businesses. So favourably were Matsushita's views received that he became popularly known in his lifetime as 'god of management'.

Matsushita was clear in his mind that corporations of all sizes are public institutions. Although corporations may legally be privately owned, their use of society's money, land and people makes them *de facto* public entities, obligated to society. When managers and employees come to the realization that a company is run not for private profit, but to improve the lives of everyone in society, including its own employees, they will have a heightened sense of mission that will lead to a stronger company.

It is tempting to polarize this division over the end of business between the US and Japan (with Asia and Europe somewhere in the middle). But there have always been business leaders in the West who, in the final analysis, perceived that business needed an end beyond making profits – or 'increasing shareholder value' as it is now sometimes called. Henry Ford – a man who you might say personified cut-throat capitalism – once declared: 'A business that is in the business of making only money is a poor kind of business.'

The end of business can be qualified as a *social* end but it is not necessary to define it any further in general terms. How a particular business acts as a means to achieving that social end depends on its changing circumstances which are as varied and unique as any general will encounter during a military operation. But having the 'next level up' end in clear view does enable a business strategic leader the better to balance the interests of the various 'stakeholders' in the enterprise: shareholders, staff, customers, suppliers, pensioners, local community, the natural environment and government as the elected leadership of the community-at-large.

As one chief executive of an international once said to me, 'A sense of service is essential. It is one of the most indispensable of all the aspects of leadership. Customers, shareholders – there are many groups that are served. True leadership is the greatest service anyone can perform. My job is to inspire people in the organization about how *good we can be* not how good we are.'

CREATIVE STRATEGIC THINKING

The natural way to think strategically is to identify your *important* and *longer-term* ends and then deploy your *means*

– resources, capabilities, time and energy – to achieve the objectives that lead you like stepping-stones towards the desired result. You will notice that the setting of these intermediate targets, objectives or goals signifies that you have moved beyond strategic thinking and into strategic planning.

There is, however, a creative alternative. A cause *must* come before an effect, but there is no similar logic that says an end must come before the means. By creatively thinking about your resources and capabilities – using not just your own imagination but that of others in the organization – new intermediate ends can hatch out from the means at your disposal. But the process does take some creative thinking.

An obvious example in the business context is the development of new products from one's existing resources, which are strategic in the sense that they create *important* and *long-term* value business within the overall business. In time these can be hived off to form self-standing product/profit centres.

New uses for Disney characters

Walt Disney's vision to create what eventually became Disneyland grew from visits to amusement parks with his own daughters. He observed the parks' run-down squalor, litter and unfriendly employees, and the boredom of the parents. Furthermore, he sensed a need among tourists for something to see when they visited Hollywood. In a 1948 memo, he sketched out plans for what he tentatively called Mickey Mouse Park:

> The Main Village, which includes the Railroad Station, is built around a village green or informal park. In the park will be benches, a bandstand, drinking fountain, trees and shrubs. It will be a place for people to sit and rest;

mothers and grandmothers can watch over small children at play. I want it to be very relaxing, cool and inviting.

Disney had a *means* at his disposal – the Disney characters and their fantastic worlds as created in the films. What he came up with was a new *end* to which they could be profitably put – entertaining visits in Disneyland theme parks.

J. A. Conger, The Charismatic Leader (San Francisco: Jossey-Bass, 1989) and B. Thomas, Walt Disney (New York: Simon & Schuster, 1976)

With creative strategic thinking it is essential to draw upon the whole 'collective wisdom' of the organization, which is not confined to those in operational or team leadership roles. Here you can use the Internet or intranet system to good advantage. As one chief executive said, 'Information technology is wonderful because it makes rich exchanges possible without formal structures.' When he took over as chief executive he told me that he had invited everyone in the company to email him with suggestions for the strategy that the company should adopt in order to regain its premier position in the industry. The response from staff of all levels and responsibilities was so great that he had to abandon his original intention to reply personally to each email, though he renewed his pledge to read every one himself.

THE NEED FOR FLEXIBILITY

It is not enough just to have vision – to see the end or desired result clearly. This must be translated into all the specific statements of long-term goals and medium-term objectives, strategic options, detailed plans, action programmes and budgets that are necessary to make the vision a living reality which is 'owned' at every level of the organization.

This strategic planning process is done differently in every organization and, in large multi-produce multi-national companies, it still tends to be an immensely complex and time-consuming process involving managers at every level of the organization.

The best course for a strategic leader today is to delegate as much as possible of this process to the operational leaders – the heads of the chief parts that make up the whole. Be an architect rather than a master builder. You should always be able to write your strategic directions in the format of a few broad goals on a piece of paper the size of this page. Encourage others further down the organization to propose other objectives, while creating an expectation that more should be allowed to emerge as things progress.

What your broad goals should do is to define the strategic direction of the organization, so that operational leaders work out their own plans and objectives – and propose others – in the light of that flight path. Some 'one-liners', as Sir John Harvey-Jones used to call them – simple directives to particular parts of the organization or, in a federal set-up, to organizations within the group – may provide all the focus that an operational leader with vision, *phronesis*, creativity and an entrepreneurial spirit needs. If he or she just cannot translate the score into great music, they should not be heading up the strings or woodwinds. Look for replacements. It is not your job to lead the violins.

Actually, immensely complex strategic plans are not a good idea, because they offend the principle of flexibility. Here is a parable:

Von Schlieffen was a Prussian Chief of General Staff who died in 1913, but his eponymous plan, revised and

updated by his successor, lived on after him. It was an
elaborate plan for mobilizing and deploying great armies
against France and Russia, using the railway network.
France would be knocked out first in a lightning campaign
through neutral Belgium to outflank the Maginot Line.
Then reinforcements would be sent by train to apply
decisive force against Russia. At the eleventh hour in 1914,
however, the autocrat of Germany, Kaiser Wilhelm,
decided that he only wanted a war against Russia, not
France or its ally Britain. His Prussian Chief-of-Staff, von
Moltke, declared that it was now quite impossible to
change the plan. All the railway timetables were fixed
towards a war against either France and Russia, or no war
at all. The Kaiser eventually gave in. By 1918 over 20
million people had lost their lives as a result.

The trouble with the Schlieffen Plan was that it lacked
flexibility. Strategy, as the *product* of a mind or minds, once
incarnated as a plan, is like any other artistic product – a
book, or poem, a musical composition – in that it can take
on a life of its own quite independent of its creator. If the
umbilical cord of strategic thinking is cut, the strategic *plan*
may soon become out of date or inappropriate in some form
or another.

As a famous general once said, 'A plan is a very good basis
for changing your mind.' When it comes to strategic planning, keep the plan as simple as possible, so that it can easily
be modified if circumstances demand it. Second, if there are
obvious contingencies – something liable to happen as an
adjunct to the planned course of action or a possible situation that can be foreseen – build them into the plan. For
unforeseen contingencies make sure that you have something
in reserve, just as a wise general always keeps some units out
of the first encounter. If the plan itself proves unworkable

for really unforeseeable reasons – not the ones you should have foreseen but overlooked or ignored – have a Plan B ready to fall back on.

Flexibility begins in the mind. It should characterize the way you think strategically, not merely the downstream activity of drawing up plans. There is a balance to be struck between flexibility and not abandoning carefully thought-out plans or courses of action lightly. It is a matter of judgement. But it helps to remember that flexibility is essentially about *means* and not about the *end* in view. You should be flexible about means, especially if the differences between them are inconsequential. As the Chinese proverb says: 'It matters not if a cat is black or white as long as it catches mice.'

Some people confuse flexibility with weakness. There is a tradition that emphasizes the strength and indomitable will-power of the individual leader. A strong leader who perseveres without a second thought down the path he or she is committed to after the course has changed is perceived as weak. Even if compelled to change course, a 'strong' leader denies it has happened to avoid the feared accusation of weakness. But such thinking betrays a misconception of strength. It is quite possible to be both flexible and firm.

Field Marshal Slim in his Sheffield lecture on leadership (1948) emphasized the quality of *flexibility of mind* as 'more and more important to leadership'. He continued:

We have found that tremendously so in the Army, because the world in material and scientific matters has advanced so much. As soon as you get into any position of command, you find yourself surrounded by new and changing factors. What it was right to do yesterday may well be wrong today; some scientific invention, some new process or political change may have come along overnight and you have got to adjust yourself and your organization to it. After all, it is the organism which can adjust itself to changed conditions which survives. This quality of flexibility of mind is increasingly vital. Time and again you will see in leaders a conflict between flexibility of mind and strength of will. I have known fellows who were very good commanders in many ways – I have served them and under them – who had strength of will but who translated it into refusal to change their minds or to receive suggestions from outside, whether from above or below. I have seen commanders who had such flexibility of mind that they always agreed with the chap they spoke to last. You have to hold this balance between flexibility of mind and strength of will, to watch that your strength of will does not become just obstinacy, that your flexibility of mind does not become vacillation. Every man must work this balance out for himself. One word of warning: if you go about reminding yourself that you are a strong man you'd better take a good look at yourself; there's something wrong.

One of the strengths of Japanese management has been broad-brush and long-term thinking, matched with considerable flexibility over means. Whereas Western management beliefs tend to portray a decision as fixed and final, Eastern philosophical tradition emphasizes individual accommodation to a continuously unfolding set of events. Indeed, faced with an obstruction, the Japanese often see the best solution as being to trace a way around it with a light touch, enough to get a trickle flowing. Let the flow of events do the rest of the work.

Yet it is important that a strategic plan should not be too formless or inchoate. It has to be explicit to be effective and specific enough to require some actions and exclude others.

KEY POINTS: GETTING THE STRATEGY RIGHT

- Strategy is a military concept by origin. Its transfer to the business field – and to organizational life more generally – was attended by much muddled thinking and misconception about it.

- *Strategia* or strategy is the art of the leader-in-chief. Strategy in the narrower sense is the thinking appropriate to the strategic leader and applies to all aspects of his or her responsibility. As it calls for above-average *phronesis* or practical wisdom – intelligence, experience and goodness – it cannot be taught like a science or skill, but like any art it can be learned by those who have an aptitude for it.

- Strategic thinking should be distinguished from strategic planning. It is essentially one form of *end-and-means* (as opposed, for example, to *cause-and-effect*). The only difference from daily common-sense considerations of end-and-means ('Shall I catch the train or fly to Paris?') is that the ends in question are *important* and *longer-term*.

- Strategy as a thing (or set of things) you can be taught to implement in generic situations does not exist. But there are *strategic ideas* in any field that are worth learning, together with historical studies of how they were applied.

- Some of these strategic ideas are fashions, but others survive the tests of time and become *principles* in their fields. The wisest strategic leaders often have a philosophy, a sketch map that helps them to identify rapidly the essentials in a very complex situation. They know what are the simple questions to ask.

- You should always be able to think one level up from a strategic *end* – which is the next higher level to which it is a *means*? Generals, for example, pursue military ends that are means to a political end. Business leaders serve ends (profitable growth, etc.) that are means to a *social* end.

- Means can be seen as creative resources and capabilities, throwing up new ends. In creative strategic thinking of this kind, it is essential that members of an organization, not just those in senior leadership roles, can themselves think creatively and strategically.

- Strategic thinking leads to strategic planning. At corporate level, the key step is to identify and communicate the 'one-liner' directives. Then it's a two-way interaction – top down and bottom out – to thrash out the actual strategic plan.

- Planning is a process not a destination. The golden rule is flexibility of mind, so that you can adapt after the plan but *still make forward progress* as circumstances unfold.

- Therefore it makes sense to keep your plans as simple as possible. Be as clear as possible about the direction that is forward or progressive. For complex plans are difficult to change at short notice. See yourself more as an architect now than a master builder.

- Your essential function here is to determine with others the direction the organization takes. The measure of your strategic thinking is whether or not it influences the way people think about what is possible, desirable and necessary.

Vision is the art of seeing things invisible.
Jonathan Swift, Irish author and satirist

8

CHANGING THE ORGANIZATIONAL CULTURE

'Changing things is central to leadership. Changing
them before anyone else is creative leadership.'

Ordway Tead, US author and educator

Organizational culture is strategically important, partly as
the end in itself and partly as the means to an end – your
overall success strategy. What is certain is that it will need to
be changed, for a culture that is static is already moribund.

Change, however, is a very broad concept. It embraces
any variation, whether affecting a thing superficially or
essentially. It covers in the same word a loss of original
identity of a substitution of one thing for another and quite
trivial alterations. Indeed, *any* process of variation, slight or
great, in appearance or essence, in quality or quantity, is
signified by change.

After your First Hundred Days you should have a good
idea of what differences you want to make – the changes
that are, in your view, necessary or desirable. If you are
involved in a business organization, these may include
changes in products and marketing strategy, in the organizational structure that balances the parts and the whole, and

in the composition of the top team. But, with the fresh eye of a newcomer, you may sense the need for a deeper change, a change in 'the way we do things', and consequently in the way the organization thinks. You are now on the borders of the organizational culture, which may well be marked by KEEP OUT signs.

Earlier in this book I compared an organization to an individual person. Each organization has a set of *generic* needs – task, team and individual – whose properties and interactions I have discovered and explored over the last fifty years. Each one, however, also has a *generic* group personality, a corporate identity often traceable back to the founder-ancestor, which is as unique as an individual's DNA or fingerprints.

The John Lewis Partnership still follows the basic values of its founder, John Speedon Lewis. McDonalds base their operation on the explicit values of Ray Kroc. Sam Walton built Wal-Mart into the world's largest retailer from a single discount store. His values still dominate the business: frugality, hands-on management, value for money and an unswerving dedication to his staff: 'If you want the people in the stores to take care of the customers, you have to make sure you're taking care of the people in the stores. That's the most important single ingredient of Wal-Mart's success.'

Have you ever tried to change your own temperament or personality? If so, you will have found you cannot do it. They can be controlled or modified, but not changed essentially. Because you are you and you always will be you.

But in the case of organizations, the analogy with an individual's personality breaks down. A better one is that of a *family*. Although some genes are passed down, each generation is different. The less inbred the family, the wider this genetic variation. A family likeness may persist, at least from parents to children, but beliefs, attitudes and values may change radically even in the short span between those two generations. The family *culture*, as we might call it, will probably have some continuities but it is also something that changes organically.

The metaphor behind *culture* is the agrarian one of preparing or cultivating soil and raising crops. On that analogy, it means the act of developing the intellectual and moral faculties, and especially improvement by education. By extension it also applies to a particular stage of advancement in civilization, and the characteristic features of such a form, state or type. We use it more loosely to describe the behaviour typical of an organization, group or task. In fact, *culture* is wider than behaviour: it embraces the distinctive customs, achievements, products, outlook, values and beliefs of a society or group – its way of life.

Going back to the agrarian metaphor, the organizational field you are contemplating has wheat and weeds growing in it. The art of changing the culture is to keep the wheat and encourage its growth while rooting out the weeds. When you take charge of an organization, you may notice a 'weed' in the culture, which needs to be addressed immediately as it could jeopardize the organization's very survival if it is in a crisis situation.

UNDERSTANDING VALUES

In the case study on page 38, Field Marshal Montgomery was addressing one aspect of organizational culture – what he called *atmosphere*. He could equally have described it as *morale*, the attitude of the army to the task in hand. Morale can fluctuate like the weather, and an effective strategic leader knows how to restore and build it up. But *climate*, as opposed to *atmosphere*, is a much more deep-seated pattern of weather. It can be changed, as we know to our cost in the phenomenon of global warming, but it is a taller order. Climate is much more akin to what is now commonly called organizational culture.

One tool you have as a strategic leader is the concept of *values*. Originally the concept of value came from the market-place and meant a fair or satisfactory equivalent or return. In the plural, *values* signify the principles or moral standards of a person, group or organization: what is considered to be valuable or important. The assumption is that these are basic beliefs and convictions that govern behaviour.

Values are abstract – you cannot see them and it is sometimes tempting to believe (or act) as if they do not exist until the keel of your ship strikes a submerged iceberg of a neglected value.

A key distinction must be made between *espoused* and *real* values. An individual or an organization may profess values as beliefs, but not live them. Actual behaviour does not match up to the espoused values. As the poet T. S. Eliot wrote, 'Between the idea and the reality, there falls a shadow.'

The dissonance between theory and practice should not be lightly interpreted as hypocrisy – play-acting – although it could well prove to be that. Hypocrisy is the robe that vice steals from virtue to mask its true nature. The test is what action the individual or organization takes when the shortfall is pointed out. Integrity will acknowledge the fault and put it right.

Apart from acting as standards and criteria for evaluating our own behaviour and that of others, values serve to stimulate or discourage certain ways of behaving. Moreover, values held in common among people provide an enduring bond, forming them into teams and communities. These values will find many expressions in the common life – political, social, economic and legal attitudes, traditions, customs, conventions and laws. Values therefore underlie our everyday relationships with each other.

Almost everything can be expressed in terms of values. For example, the relations between parts and whole in an organization – decentralization versus centralization – can reflect the values of *freedom* and *order*.

One advantage of thinking about values is that it helps to simplify the complexity of life. The Greek mind searched for the simple and generic amidst complexity – the search for the elements that make up nature illustrate that tendency. They thought there were four – earth, fire, air and water – but we know there to be not less than a hundred elements. But it was the Greeks who first introduced that key concept of an *element*. In the field of values, we owe them the identification and naming some of the 'elements' or basic values we know today, not least the sublime trinity of *good, truth* and *beauty*.

The source of these essential values, and how they relate to each other, are metaphysical issues. Strategic leaders aim to be pragmatists – their vocation is *practical* wisdom. For a leader, what matters most about values is that they function like stars in our lives, individually or corporately, providing a guidance which is qualitatively different from the direction we gain from maps, charts or sets of rules. By values, whether consciously or on automatic pilot, we navigate ourselves through life.

PROVIDING DIRECTION THROUGH VISION AND VALUES

Values is a term that works well in everyday life without definition, for we all know what it means. But if you think a significant change of culture is called for, you have to examine your organization's values. Or, more precisely, invite the organization to do it. There are two questions that you need to ask:

> What are our values now?
> What should our values be in x years' time?

(What x equals depends upon a variety of factors, such as the degree of crisis, the size and history of the organization in question. It must be far enough away to be realistic in terms of cultural change and near enough to be real, exciting and challenging.)

With email, technology can give everyone in the organization the opportunity to contribute to the discussions. You should personally lead the discussion of these questions at board and top executive team levels, and expect the operational leaders to do the same with their senior teams.

What should emerge is a profile of about ten dominant *characteristics* that govern the present culture, unerringly reflecting its underlying values. You should also have a list of the characteristics of tomorrow's organization, the fruits of the practical wisdom that all staff (not just leaders) possess in more abundance than many so-called strategic leaders conceive. It is the one resource that managers neglect at their peril.

When you and your colleagues compare the two lists you may notice that some characteristics – for example, a *reputation for excellent craftsmanship* – appears on both lists. These characteristics or values are the pearls on the necklace of continuity. Other characteristics – for instance, *over-cautious and risk-averse* or *conservative and hostile to change* – have mysteriously disappeared. Well, disappeared off the list. But how do you actually substitute a new value, behaviour and attitude, such as *bold but prudent entrepreneurial spirit*, or *a positive willingness to change*, in place of these tired and due-for-retirement characteristics?

There are three courses open to you, and you should follow them all: communication, example and system. Let us consider each in turn.

If you have conducted an exercise along the lines of the one I have sketched here, you have already begun not only that process, but also the equally important one of getting commitment to change and 'ownership' of it. The next obvious step is to write down and circulate throughout the organization a statement of the *vision* of tomorrow's organization that has emerged, together with the consistent *values* that give it body, colour and shape.

Common sense supports you in taking this step, but do not expect too much of it. First, whatever you write down is a snapshot photograph of your thinking today – it will evolve and change. The remedy for that potential objection is to build in a review date. Second, the chief benefit is derived to those who actually *write* the statement of vision and values, for writing does involve thinking. Receiving a paper, perusing it or even reading it, doesn't necessarily involve the thought process. The fate of many organizational 'mission statements' is to be filed away and eventually forgotten. How do you write the vision and values on people's hearts?

Granted that a written summary is part of your strategy, there is an art in doing it. Here are the principles:

- The statement should be brief but specific. Ideally it should be contained upon one side of A4 paper. Such a succinct statement can then be better communicated with the various intended audiences, through such means as inclusion in company reports or plastic cards that people can keep in their pockets.

- It should contain a clear vision of what type of organization is being created for the future. A short, clear sentence encapsulating the essence of the organization should head the page.
- This unifying vision of what the organization is being built for tomorrow should be creative, exciting and achievable so as to gain commitment from all its members. Dreams should be excluded.
- The more detailed sections should spell out how this is going to be achieved. These will include some broad strategic directions, such as a definition of the business the company *will be in* (not necessarily *is in*).
- The body of the statement should always contain a section that sets out clearly the moral or ethical values and *will* guide the organization in the future, whatever may have been the case in the past.

You will notice that touches of strategic thinking come into an effective statement of vision and values. The reason is that purpose and organization in their broadest senses cannot be divorced (as the three circle model reminds us). The vision of what kind of organization is being built, and what its key values are, is inextricably interwoven with its core purpose and the strategy that will thereby be more effectively fulfilled. Each of the values or characteristics listed should be justifiable in terms of the reason why the organization exists and where it intends to position itself within its field. That is not to say that some values – for example, the value of the individual person or of the environment – may not be ends in themselves, but they are also means to ends as well, as far as creating a better organization is concerned.

Konosuke Matsushita exemplified this approach. A sound leadership vision in terms of broad direction and values was the chief article in his philosophy of management. Manpower, technology, funding, plant and equipment are important to management, but it is even more important, Matsushita believed, that the chief executive should set up sound company goals and ideas and make sure that all his employees are thoroughly acquainted and in agreement with them. Such a philosophy is the foundation on which all other elements can be made to work.

The key to the Japanese success was 'management by collective wisdom'. Matsushita and his contemporaries in such firms as Sony, Toyota and Mitsubishi held that no matter how good a manager is, his knowledge and abilities are limited. Every employee actively involved in management, freely giving of his or her ideas and innovations, is an indispensable factor in the corporate process.

To that end of involving the hearts and minds of all to achieve the corporate vision, most Japanese companies have either a *shaze* or a *shakun* – or both. *Sha* means company, *ze* means what is right or justified, *kun* means precept. Therefore *shaze* is a tersely expressed statement, in lofty high-sounding, formalized language, of corporate ideals and principles, whereas *shakun* is in the same form but directed at a company employee, tends to be expressed in ordinary language.

The original is usually written in brush calligraphy, framed and hung up in the president's office or the board conference room. In some Japanese companies it is still customary to recite in unison the *shaze* or *shakun* every morning before starting work, as part of the *chorei* – the inspirational briefing that often begins the week or even the working day. It may last only a few minutes but it helps to create a 'let's go' state of mind and a feeling of identity with the team.

LIVING THE VISION

Because example is so integral to leadership at any level, it crops up in every chapter of this book! Here it is again: it is no good just sending out a piece of paper with your corporate vision and values inscribed on it – you and your colleagues in leadership roles must *live the vision and the values*. That doesn't imply that you should be perfect – shortcomings and shortfalls are human and inevitable. But acknowledge conduct or behaviour that falls below the standards you have incised with lapidary clarity on the corporate tablets of stone, make amends *and try again*. It is only by making real in your own life what you and the top team expect from others, that they will be able to *see* the new order and not merely *read* it.

Make sure, too, that the systems in the organization that have to do with the selecting and training of people, how their objectives are set and their performance appraised, reinforce the communication of vision and values. If your organization *rewards* people for being over-cautious, don't expect them to become bolder and more innovative. If the system decapitates those who make errors, don't be surprised if people never stick their necks out – even if great opportunities float by.

You do not get creativity, however, without individuality, and that in turn means resolutely giving people the licence of *freedom* within the broad framework of *order*. To be deviants – to be those who differ markedly from the group norms, the established ways, the ideas and assumptions that govern the majority – is often a necessary condition for being creative (not a sufficient one, however, for many deviants are disruptive, antisocial and unconstructive).

GETTING THE PACE OF CHANGE RIGHT

Changing the organizational culture is a very slow business in an organization which has a culture adverse to change. 'Do I really *have* to change?' is the silent cry. Of course, if an organization *has* to change, it will – at the last minute, truculently and with many a complaint. When panic really sets in, the response to change suddenly switches from '*Over my dead body*' to '*Let's do it overnight*'.

Abraham Lincoln used to tell a story about a frog that fell into a deep, muddy wagon track. A couple of days later, he was still there. Frog friends found him and urged him to get out of his predicament. He made a few feeble efforts, but remained mired in his rut.

For the next few days, his friends kept encouraging him to try harder, but they finally gave up and went back to their pond.

The next day the frog was seen sunning himself contentedly beside the edge of the pond.

'How did you get out of the rut?' his friends asked.

'Well, as you know,' said the frog, 'I couldn't, but a wagon came along and I *had* to.'

The problem with Lincoln's frog is that inordinate delay in changing left him only one option. As a general principle, the sooner an organization is willing to change – ahead, that is, of the time it *has* to change – the more options it has open to it. Instead of being forced, change becomes proactive in nature and aimed at securing the heights of advantage.

By changing *ahead of time* you gain some solid advantages. Most organizations in any field have a herd instinct: they stick close together and only change when they are following suit or catching up. Organizations that are leaders in their field (is that not in *your* vision?) are pioneers – they change first before necessity or competitive interest compels them to do so in varying degrees of reluctance. It is always better to take change by the hand and lead it where you want it to go before it takes you by the throat and drags you in any direction.

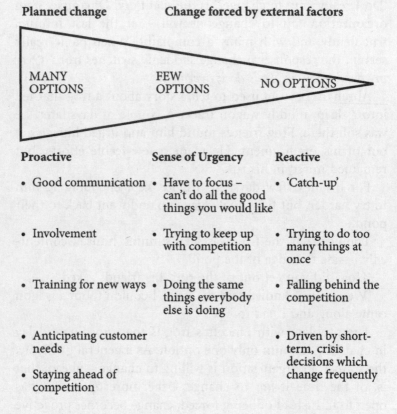

Planned change	Change forced by external factors	
MANY OPTIONS	FEW OPTIONS	NO OPTIONS
Proactive	**Sense of Urgency**	**Reactive**
• Good communication	• Have to focus – can't do all the good things you would like	• 'Catch-up'
• Involvement	• Trying to keep up with competition	• Trying to do too many things at once
• Training for new ways	• Doing the same things everybody else is doing	• Falling behind the competition
• Anticipating customer needs		• Driven by short-term, crisis decisions which change frequently
• Staying ahead of competition		

Planned change versus change forced by external factors

The necessity to change ahead of a Lincoln's frog jump, and the change that is both necessary or desirable in terms of vision and values, should form your major theme as a communicator.

Standing up and addressing meetings as Montgomery did before Alamein, issuing short statements on paper, talking informally with groups, having conversations with individuals – these are all 'moments of truth' when you can share your message and listen, as part of your overall strategy of communication.

One common mistake is to believe that communicating the broad aims, values or ideals of the organization can be done on video or down-line. Research confirms that tele-communication of this sort is rarely effective except as a back-up. Face-to-face communication, preferably in small groups, cannot be beaten when it comes to changing the organizational culture.

The transformation of managers into business leaders constitutes the core of every success story in bringing about organizational change – *there are no exceptions*. There is no other way to lead a global organization except by the leadership of a vision and values which all serve, including the chief executives. Self-discipline is the only way to reconcile those two apparent opposites, *order* and *freedom*. If I freely and willingly accept *order*, I remain *free*. Offering a person a vision and a set of values, which reason accepts and the heart affirms, is now the best way to provide strategy direction.

'People think I am some kind of giant who is everywhere,' one chief executive told me. 'Not so, it's a question of making values known and accepted by hundreds of senior managers. This is also important when it comes to recruiting, keeping and promoting talented people. I have to convince them to be business leaders. We are in an industry with a good population of bright people, at least 25,000 to 30,000 with academic degrees. You have to bring the right people in, give them the mission, then mobilize them.

'Every organization needs values,' he continued, 'but a

lean organization needs them even more. When you strip away the support system of staffs and layers, people need to change their habits and expectations or else the stress will just overwhelm them ... *values are what enable people to guide through that kind of change.*'

KEY POINTS: CHANGING THE ORGANIZATIONAL STRUCTURE

- Few strategic leaders will not be faced with the challenge of changing the corporate culture of the organization they head. Culture is not the same as structure, which is relatively easy to change. It is the deeper-seated pattern – unique to every organization – of assumptions, beliefs, attitudes, habit and customs.

- The concept of *values*, which came into wider currency as a substitute for *ideals* some fifty years ago, is a useful way of expressing a culture. 'An institution is the lengthened shadow of one man,' said Emerson. Values are often the cultural genes of the founder.

- One proven way to initiate or further corporate change is to list the ten adjectives that *characterize* the organization now, and the ten that should characterize it in *x* years' time. The values that appear on both lists is your *continuity*; the new arrivals are indicators of change.

- As part of a strategy for change, it makes sense more often than not to produce a short written statement of vision and values. Together they should provide all members and stakeholders with a clear and consistent picture of the longer-term state and the character of the organization.

- Do not expect such a statement to be effective by itself. It needs to be communicated and discussed in small group meetings at every level. Not just by words – live the vision and values yourself and expect your colleagues to do the same.

- The cluster of beliefs and attitudes that facilitate or retard change is critical in any corporate culture. In any age where the accelerating pace of change calls for speedier response times, organizations that are changing 'proactively' rather than 'reactively' will always have a competitive advantage.
- Central to all corporate renewal is one necessity: you have to transform your managers into business leaders at all operational and team levels. For only leadership by example – leaders who lead the way instead of talking about it – can unlock the hidden greatness in the organization.

> *Do not, as some ungracious pastors do,*
> *Show me the steep and thorny way to heaven,*
> *Whiles, like a puff'd and reckless libertine,*
> *Himself the primrose path of dalliance treads,*
> *And recks not his own rede [advice].*
> William Shakespeare, English poet and playwright

9

FINDING TIME
FOR INDIVIDUALS

*'Not geniuses, but average men require profound
stimulation, incentive towards creative effort, and
the nurture of great hopes.'*
John Collier, British author and screenplay writer

However great their responsibilities, strategic leaders only
have twenty-four hours in a day like everyone else. 'If only I
had more time' is a natural feeling which besets all busy
people, and who in these days is not busy? Yet we shall never
have any more time. We have, and we have always had, all
the time there is. 'Those who make the worst use of their
time are the first to complain of its brevity,' said the French
seventeenth-century moralist Jean de la Bruyère.

Time, then, is your scarcest resource. It is irreplaceable
and irreversible. Few things are more important to a strategic
leader than learning how to save time and how to spend it
wisely. For the 'time bill' of strategic leadership within the
organization is a high one. Each of the four preceding
chapters will have carried that message home. Moreover, on
becoming a strategic leader you move out of the engine
room and on to the bridge. A large amount of your time will

be spent 'outside the egg' of the organization as such. That may entail travelling to meet major customers, relating to major allies, or being away in connection with mergers or acquisitions. Then you need to spend time out of the organization, keeping up to speed on what's going on in your own field, or investing time in growing in stature as a strategic leader. For many shrink while in office as strategic leaders. As Dag Hammarskjöld, the Swedish statesman and former Secretary-General of the United Nations put it: 'Time goes by; reputation increases, ability declines.'

To these time-calls we must add any strategic leader's core or generic function (see page 84) of managing the interface of the organization with society as a whole – the sea on which the organization moves. It's a two-way process: society impacts with fresh demands, expectations and values on the organization; the organization has a potentially positive or negative effect on society.

To these work-related demands must be added the modern expectation (and desire) to spend much more time with one's family than earlier generations of corporate leaders. Duty, yes, but let it not eclipse the values of family life. It is a balance that, in effect, does cut down *some* of the time we are prepared to devote to work.

The strategic leader who allows him or herself to be overwhelmed by the sheer avalanche of demands on their time soon ceases to be a leader and resorts to being a manager, executive or administrator. The urgent drives out the important, the short-term triumphs over the long-term, and so strategic thinking goes out of the window. The vision and values that shone before you like stars at the end of the First Hundred Days' honeymoon, are now merely words on paper, filed away for attention at some further date 'when we have more time'. You are too busy to spend time – real time – with individuals, even key operational leaders.

How do you avoid this common fate? You can start with either the 'supply' side or the 'demand' side of the equation. On the 'supply' side, the key question is: how can you release as much discretionary time as possible – that is, time that you can choose to spend as you wish? On the 'demand' side, the matching question is really about what you are being paid to do:

Achieving the task	Strategic thinking, planning and implementation – making it happen.
Building the team	Not just the top team but teamwork – based on a just balance of whole and parts – as the other face of the coin of organization.
Developing the individual	Helping individuals to grow and to make their maximum contribution.

As I have already written fully on the *task* and *team* broad functional circles of responsibility, I shall focus in this chapter on the *individual* one – your function as a leader in that key area. But first there is the issue of how to make the time available for all those key responsibilities, not least time for individuals – so often at the bottom of the manager's list of priorities. That takes us to the 'supply' side – the call to become an excellent manager of your time.

THE TEN PRINCIPLES OF TIME MANAGEMENT

In a companion book to this one – *Effective Time Management* – I suggested that there are ten key principles of time management. Under each heading I explored the 'how-to-do-it' aspects of the subject. Rather than going over the same ground here, I shall use the framework to remind you of what you as a chief executive should be doing strategically to make the best use of your time. For I am assuming that you have long since mastered the tactics of the subject.

1 Develop a personal sense of time

> But at my back I always hear
> Time's wingèd chariot hurrying near.

Like Andrew Marvell in these words from 'To His Coy Mistress' (1650), you should remind your 'mistress' – the organization – that your days as a strategic leader are numbered. You cannot afford to waste your own time or allow others to waste it, wittingly or unwittingly. That doesn't mean, however, that you become a kind of time miser, grudging every minute. The object is to be able to spend time freely, generously and spontaneously. You have heard of 'value for money' – get 'value for time'.

2 Identify long-term goals

Your work of identifying the *ends* of your strategic thinking and expressing them in simple terms of vision, four or five open-ended aims and a set of defining values – all in a single unified concept of the kind of organization you are there to bring into being during your term of stewardship – is immensely important as a guiding principle for how you should be spending your own time.

3 Make middle-term plans

Organizationally, this is the realm of strategic planning: establishing the goals and objectives – specific, time-bounded, realistic, stretching and exciting – which are the concrete destinations, like towns and cities, the chief parts of the organization need to achieve on the road forwards that your long-term thinking has identified.

On the personal level, you can apply this principle by setting yourself five or six (not more) goals or objectives as part of the agreed general strategy and distinct from what the operational leaders have committed themselves to achieving. This personal profile of objectives for completion in three to five years may well become clear to you during the First Hundred Days. For example, a personal objective might be to identify the right successor, from within or outside the organization, to take over the helm.

4 Plan the day

An excellent personal assistant (and supporting staff in a large organization) is essential for any strategic leader. With such a PA it is comparatively easy to work out a system for managing the diary. Reviewing the week ahead together makes sense at any level of time management.

Like any plan, flexibility is essential. If you have to make changes, remember that it is essential that you personally, or your PA, explain to those affected the reasons for doing so, and of course make the necessary arrangements.

5 Make the best use of your time

Reserve high-quality time – usually early in the morning – for thinking time. By that I don't mean necessarily being on your own. Solitude and thinking are linked, but you will have plenty of solitude while travelling, for example, or at odd times of the day like a free lunch hour, or at home during the weekends, doing some gardening or driving about. Thinking time in strategic leadership involves others, either a small group or individuals. What matters, however, is that subjects which demand creativity, wisdom or imagination are not left as an afterthought at the end of a gruelling ten-hour day, or just before you are leaving for an airport.

6 Organize office work

You need an office staff to handle your affairs, and a room where you can work quietly on your own and hold meetings with small groups (round table to be preferred) or individuals (comfortable chairs round a coffee table). But the less time you spend in your office the better. When asked why he was so rarely behind his desk, the president of Toyota replied, 'We do not make cars in my office.'

The skills of handling the inevitable paperwork and emails, filtered and placed in simple categories by your PA, are covered in *Effective Time Management*. The key is to be able to spot the simple issues in the complexity of the written word. It is a matter of isolating the essentials.

As a general policy, if a paper requires a decision from you the relevant issues, features or information should be set out and the person or committee submitting the paper – having identified the courses of action open – should make their recommendation. In other words, get them to bring you solutions rather than naked problems.

7 Manage meetings

Meetings should begin on time and end on time. Your skills as a leader of meetings need to be well honed, for you will find yourself chairing plenty of them. If you can be brisk and businesslike, yet gracious and courteous, the business gets done and people will look forward to your meetings.

There is no rule that says meetings should be unenjoyable but hilarious ones are usually unproductive.

Your main concern at a meeting should be for the quality of the thinking displayed there. For the process of gathering and sifting the collective wisdom – the leadership of ideas – creates judgement. Only decisions based on sound judgement are likely to be good ones, and so the preliminary thinking needs to be as rigorous as you can make it.

8 Delegate effectively

The Golden Rule of time management for strategic leaders! The main candidates for delegation are the managerial parts of the role. You may recall from Chapter 4 that *strategia*, the art of being a commander-in-chief or equivalent, includes responsibility for the day-to-day operations of an organization and its sustainability in terms of logistics and administration. As there are plenty of people who both like doing this sort of work and are better at doing it than you are, why not let them do it? That frees you up for what you are being paid for – strategic leadership.

Yet delegation should never generate into abdication, the vice of mentally slothful senior managers. You should have a passion for good administration and really value those who deliver it, just as Abraham Lincoln esteemed Stanton for doing so (see page 121).

The mistake some strategic leaders make is to delegate only what they don't want to do themselves! If you see delegation as a means of developing your colleagues and not merely as a way of reducing your own workload, offer them some demanding and challenging tasks – things you would really like to do yourself if time allowed.

9 Make use of committed time

Julius Caesar dictated to five secretaries who accompanied him on horseback as he rode on his campaigns – his equivalent of a mobile phone. Travel time is especially useful to a strategic leader because it does allow time to think. Nowadays, however, the mobile phone, useful tool as it is, brings interruptions even into travel time, unless you are minded to switch it off.

Waiting time – for example, when someone is unavoidably late for a meeting in your room – gives you some minutes to check a letter or read a paper. During a busy day, committed time does yield these pockets – five minutes here, ten minutes there – which can all be put to use. *Look after the minutes and the hours will look after themselves.*

10 Manage your health

Being a strategic leader in today's changing world is a demanding role: you need to be mentally and physically fit. Energy, vitality and resilience can only be sustained by adequate sleep, temperance and taking sensible exercise.

How do you stay *mentally fit*? Use your brain in spheres outside the organization, in related or unrelated interests that call for the exercise of the mind. The simplest and most time-efficient way of doing this is to read books. Not for information – use the Internet for that – but because they invite you to think, reflect and keep things in perspective.

CASE STUDY: LIEUTENANT-GENERAL SIR BRIAN HORROCKS

Lieutenant-General Sir Brian Horrocks commanded 13 Corps, a group of armoured divisions, under Montgomery at the crucial battle of Alam Halfa on 31 August 1942, when Rommel made his final attempt to win Egypt. Horrocks's troops took the brunt of the attack and within three days the thrust had been defeated. In his memoirs, *A Full Life* (1960), he recounted this sequel:

> On the day after the battle (Alam Halfa) I was sitting in my headquarters purring with satisfaction. The battle had been won and I had not been mauled in the process. What could be better? Then in came a liaison officer from Eighth Army headquarters bringing me a letter in Monty's even hand. This is what he said:
>
> > Dear Horrocks,
> > Well done – but you must remember that you are now a corps commander and not a divisional commander . . .
>
> He went on to list four or five things which I had done wrong, mainly because I had interfered too much with the tasks of my subordinate commanders. The purring stopped abruptly. Perhaps I wasn't quite such a heaven-sent general after all. But the more I thought over the battle, the more I realized that Monty was right. So I rang him up and said, 'Thank you very much.'
> I mention this because Montgomery was one of the few commanders who tried to train the people who worked under him. Who else, on the day after his first major victory, which had altered the whole complexion of the

war in the Middle East, would have taken the trouble to write a letter like this in his own hand to one of his subordinate commanders?

Not long after the following battle at Alamein, while preparing for the final offensive in Tunisia, Horrocks was gravely wounded while in the forward area. After a year in hospital, soon after D-Day, he took command of thirty corps on the Normandy beaches – once more under Montgomery – and put into practice the lessons he had learned at Alam Halfa.

A LEADER OF LEADERS

What Montgomery was doing, as we can all recognize, amounted to 'on-the-job' training in strategic leadership for one of his senior operational leaders now in a strategic leadership role. Hedged between two great battles only days apart, Montgomery both found the time to do it – time management – and did so directly and effectively. Horrocks, for his part, had great respect for Montgomery – 'He was obviously a complete master of his craft, the craft of war' – and he had the humility to see that he had much to learn about giving his divisional commanders direction and freedom.

The same theatre of operations in the Second World War gives us another compelling example of an exceptionally burdened strategic leader finding time to teach leadership on a one-to-one basis and in the context of an actual situation. Auchinleck, who had succeeded Wavell as Middle East Commander-in-Chief, was a diffident, reserved and rather remote man. In a memo dated 29 November 1941 and headed 'Personal and Secret', Churchill urged Auchinleck to 'visit the battlefield. Coming fresh to the scene with your drive and full knowledge of the situation you will put new vigour into the troops and inspire everyone to a supreme effort . . .' This memo did the trick, as history relates. For it was Auchinleck's visit to the front that restored confidence when the offensive against Rommel was on the point of being abandoned, and led to the stopping of Rommel's army south of Tobruk: 'the end of the beginning'.

Yet Auchinleck could not grasp the principle of why these forward visits had worked. As the war in the desert fell into the doldrums, Churchill flew out to meet him and assess the situation for himself. He sensed the morale problem in the Eighth Army, and once more urged Auchinleck to make himself familiar to the troops. The general replied that in his experience familiarity only bred contempt. 'In *my* experience,' replied Churchill, 'you cannot breed anything without familiarity.' Alexander was brought in to replace Auchinleck, and Montgomery took over the Eighth Army: 'Everyone felt that new dynamic force had entered into the tired, rather stale old body of the Eighth Army.'

The selection, support, encouragement and development of your key operational leaders – balanced by the capacity to stand back and give them the maximum freedom to achieve objectives in their own way and in their own personal style – is a core requirement in a strategic leader. You are a 'leader of leaders', as was said of Alexander the Great.

Essentially what is happening here is that you are finding time for individuals. At the core of these conversations and interchanges are the *agreeing of objectives* and the *appraising of performance*. At this level – indeed at all levels of leadership – communication is two-way. Nor is it a question of a formal interview to agree objectives and another, six months later, to do a 'performance appraisal', filling in forms and all that sort of thing. You should leave all that for the management textbooks. You should establish close and continuing contact, but on a non-interference basis. Progress-reviewing is the natural theme for these separate conversations with the chief operational leaders, but they will include a wider range of subjects – not least the ever-changing situation of the business and the field as a whole.

'A good shepherd knows his sheep.' In this way, the members of the top team get to know your mind well, just as Nelson's captains came to understand his views on the tactics to be employed in all the conceivable situations they might face. Equally, your knowledge of each individual slowly builds up, so that you are aware of each person's uniqueness – what they can do and how they choose to do it.

As Napoleon said, because of the variety of individual qualities 'in the profession of war, like that of letters, each man has his style'. Of his own generals, for example, he knew that Massena excelled in vigorous attacks, but Jourdan would be preferable in defence. Reynier, a topographical engineer, always offered sound advice, but his personality was incommunicative, cold and taciturn. Lannes was 'wise, prudent and bold', ill-educated but with natural talent and imperturbable sang-froid. Moreau was useless at *la grande guerre* but always led from the front. And so on. Napoleon knew his marshals and generals thoroughly. He did not treat them as being interchangeable, for each one was particularly suited for a certain kind of task. But, he added, a complete general – fit for all situations – 'is no common thing'.

It follows that your relationship with each individual in your team will be different. For each person will evoke a fact of your own personality which may not be touched by others. Like a parent, however, you should ensure that these relationships are essentially professional, not to be confused with friendships. For friendships grow from liking some individuals more than others, which has the corollary that you like others less. And people, not being short on discernment, will soon sense where your personal preferences lie. Who are the favoured sheep and who the unattractive goats? Avoid giving any the impression that some operational leaders are your personal friends, while others are not. That kind of perception is divisive in a team, whereas you are there to build the relationships *between* these individuals as members of a team, not merely to relate to them on a one-to-one basis like spokes on a wheel-hub. Even worse, these chief executives who indulge in 'divide-and-rule' tactics have lost touch completely with the spirit and practice of strategic leadership.

EACH INDIVIDUAL COUNTS

Field Marshal Montgomery exemplifies the strategic leader who knows how to make time to think. 'When all was confusing,' said Sir Brian Horrocks, who as one of his chief operational leaders knew Montgomery well, 'he had the supreme gift of reducing the most complex situation to simplicity. More than any other man I have ever met he was able to sit back and *think*, with the result that he was never deluded by "the trees".'

Montgomery's second great priority, as he once told me in the boardroom of St. Paul's School (see page 53), was to make the soldiers in the Eighth Army 'partners with me in the battle' – not just the headquarters staff or the unit commanders but *each* soldier. Each individual needed to know the strategic importance of what they were being asked to do and their precise part in the drama that was unfolding. By word of mouth and in writing, Montgomery used the time he had created by ruthless delegation to get across that simple message – both personally and by insuring that commanders briefed their troops properly on the strategy and tactics. As Horrocks said, speaking of the main qualities of leadership that bound the Eighth Army to its commander-in-chief, 'He took infinite pains to explain to every man in the Army exactly what was required of him.'

It all comes down to the individual

'... And they said he's a skilful commander,' rejoined Pierre.

'I don't understand what is meant by "a skilful commander",' replied Prince Andrew ironically.

'A skilful commander?' replied Pierre. 'Why, one who foresees all contingencies ... and foresees the adversary's intentions.'

'But that's impossible,' said Prince Andrew as if it were a matter settled long ago.

Pierre looked at him in surprise.

'And yet they say that war is like a game of chess?' he remarked.

'Yes,' replied Prince Andrew, 'but with this little difference, that in chess you may think over each move as long as you please and are not limited for time, and with this difference too, that a knight is always stronger than a pawn, and two pawns are always stronger than one, while in war a battalion is sometimes weaker than a company. The relative strength of bodies of troops can never be known to anyone. Believe me,' he went on, 'if things depended on arrangements made by the staff, I should be there making arrangements, but instead of that I have the honour to serve here in the regiment with these gentlemen, and I consider that on us tomorrow's battle will depend, not on those others ... Success never depends, and never will depend, on position, or equipment or even on numbers, and least of all on position.'

'But on what then?'

'On the feeling that is in me and in him,' he pointed to Timokhin, 'and each soldier . . .'

Leo Tolstoy, War and Peace (1866)

In Tripoli, after the successful 'break-through' in Alamein, Horrocks witnessed an example of the Army's affection for its commander – a standing ovation by all ranks before and after a concert party's performance.

> And here in the Eighth Army was the same outward and visible sign of the greatest battle-winning factor of all – a spirit of complete trust, confidence and affection within a formation. This sort of happy family atmosphere is common enough in divisions which have lived, trained and grown up together, but it is comparatively rare in higher formations. I know of only two in our army where it existed strongly during the last war – Montgomery's Eighth Army and Slim's Fourteenth Army. And it is significant that both men took over their commands at a time when things were going badly and morale was low.

If such strategic leadership – one that touches each individual – is rare in very large formations like armies, it is not surprising that it is so uncommon in peacetime. Size is often given as the reason by less than excellent strategic leaders. How can you communicate in Montgomery's way with each individual when, as for instance in Britain's National Health Service, there are almost one million employees? Yet Slim's Fourteenth Army was also composed of more than a million employees. If Slim could do it, why not you?

CARING FOR EACH INDIVIDUAL

As individuals we respond to those who care for us, who meet our individual needs. It is futile to expect individuals in any organization to respond by giving their best unless the organization – the leadership at all levels – demonstrates in the most practical way *that each individual matters*.

In a large organization like an army it is, of course, impossible that the strategic leader should personally care for the individual, although it is not unknown, and when it happens the effect is always powerful.

Wu Ch'i

Regard your soldiers as your children, and they will follow you into the deepest valleys; look on them as your own beloved sons, and they will stand by you even unto death. Tu Mu drew an engaging picture of the famous general Wu Ch'i:

He wore the same clothes and ate the same food as the meanest of his soldiers, refused to have either a horse to ride or a mat to sleep on, carried his own surplus rations wrapped in a parcel, and shared every hardship with his men. One of his soldiers was suffering from an abscess, and Wu Ch'i himself sucked out the virus. The soldier's mother, hearing this, began wailing and lamenting. Somebody asked her, saying: 'Why do you cry? Your son is only a common soldier, and yet the commander-in-chief himself has sucked out the poison from his sore.' The woman replied: 'Many years ago Lord Wu performed a similar service for my husband, who never left him afterwards, and finally met his death at the hands of the enemy. And now that he has done the same for my son, he too will fall fighting I know not where.'

> If, however, you are indulgent, but unable to make
> your authority felt; kind-hearted, but unable to enforce
> your commands; and incapable, moreover, of quelling
> disorder: then your soldiers must be likened to spoilt
> children; they are useful for any practical purpose.
>
> Sun Tzu, *The Art of War* (c. 500 B. C.)

Although it is the role of operation and team leaders to care
for the individual, the strategic leader still 'owns' the third
circle – 'meeting individual needs' and it is strategically
important that lower levels of leaders do actually lead in this
respect. The strategic leader should be watchful and obser-
vant, falling like a ton of bricks on those who fall short of
this basic requirement. Here are two brief examples of
strategic leaders who did just that.

Wellington

Wellington appeared to be rather remote. But he showed a
real concern for the individual wellbeing of his men.

During the Peninsular War in Spain, a guest at dinner
one evening mentioned that he had just come from a place
where a number of sick and wounded soldiers lay without
shelter, exposed to the cold.

Immediately after dinner Wellington ordered his horse.
With his aide-de-camp he rode thirty miles, arriving at
midnight to find officers comfortably installed in warm
quarters on a bitterly cold night, while the sick and wounded
lay outside exposed to the elements. He ordered the sick and
wounded to be housed and the officers to sleep outdoors.
He returned to his own headquarters before dawn.

The following evening he told his ADC that he had the
nagging suspicion that the surly officers might have dis-

obeyed his orders when his back had turned. So Wellington again rode thirty miles at night to find that the sick were indeed still in the open and the officers sleeping in warm beds in their quarters. He had the officers arrested for disobedience and cashiered.

Slim

Slim linked unselfish care for others, which he expected from his officers, with that overarching leadership virtue – integrity. It combined 'being honest with all men' and not putting self first. Integrity means 'thinking of others, the people we had, before ourselves. Moral reasons are, strangely enough, the ones that both in war and commerce tell most in the long run, but apart from its spiritual aspect this attitude – and there need be nothing soft or sloppy about it – has a practical material value. The real test of leadership is not if your men will follow you in success but if they will stick by you in defeat and hardship. They won't do that unless they believe you to be honest and to have care of them.

'I once had under me a battalion that had not done well in a fight. I went to see why. I found the men in the jungle, tired, hungry, dirty, jumpy, some of them wounded, sitting miserably about doing nothing. I looked for the CO – for any officer; none was to be seen. Then, as I rounded a bush, I realized why that battalion had failed. Collected under a tree were the officers, having a meal while the men went hungry. Those officers had forgotten the tradition of the Service that they look after their men's wants before their own. I was compelled to remind them. I hope they never again forgot the integrity and unselfishness that always permeates good leadership. I have never known men fail to respond to them.'

The principle is a simple one. If you give you will receive. Show care and solicitude for the individual and the individual will repay you a hundredfold by their service to the cause.

To establish an organization, however, which is oriented towards the individual in this way does depend on commanders who are leaders in the sense that they own and act upon *all* the three circles. In fact there is a long tradition in the British Army, as in others, that commanders are expected to be leaders. It is clear that even before the days of Nelson and Wellington officers were expected to be first and foremost leaders where it mattered most – on the field of battle. No coercion but the *willing* response of each individual is what counts.

Leading from the front is obviously a *task* activity. Like the parts of an iceberg below the surface of the water, the *team* and *individual* circles are submerged and less visible. As the stories above illustrate, however, effective military strategic leaders are not only *teambuilders* but also always show a direct and indirect (through the line of command) concern for the welfare of the *individual*.

The individual circle encompasses not only material needs for food and shelter, but the more intangible need to feel a valued part of a great and worthwhile enterprise. It is the diametric opposite to the sense of being merely a cog in an impersonal machine, an engine part to be thrown on the scrap-heap when it is broken or worn out. Of course, as individual persons – in the context of our family and friends – you and I are irreplaceable. But in the working organizational context we *are* replaceable parts, we *are* means to corporate ends. None of us is indispensable, and we should be lacking in elemental humility if we thought otherwise. But we are not *merely* means to ends. We work best when we are made to feel equals and partners, with an intrinsic worth and dignity of our own which is not lost in the organization and which we will take away with us when we leave this service.

To a young reader the Second World War may seem an age away, but seven decades are just a drop in the bucket as far as history is concerned. Computers, nuclear energy, and jet engines are but three of the technological innovations in that war which have transformed our lives. The much slower revolution we also owe to it – the transformation of management into business leadership – is only just beginning to gather momentum. But we have yet to address the major challenge of transforming managers throughout the world into leaders who achieve the *task*, build *teams* and find time for each *individual*. Slim had a clear vision of the essential difference between leadership and management, as he explained to an Australian audience in Adelaide in 1957 in a lecture that has become a classic.

General Slim on 'Leadership in Management'

The problems met at the top of any great organization, whether military or civilian, are basically the same – questions of organization, transportation, equipment, resources, the selection of men for jobs, the use of experts and, above all and through all, human relations. Now, while the problems are much alike, there are certain differences between the military and the civil approach to them and in the climates in which they have to be solved.

To begin with, we do not in the Army talk of 'management' but of 'leadership'. This is significant. There is a difference between leadership and management. The leader and the men who follow him represent one of the oldest, most natural and most effective of all human relationships. The manager and those he manages are the later product, with neither so romantic nor so inspiring a history. Leadership is of the spirit, compounded of personality and vision; its practice is an art. Management is of the mind, more a matter of accurate calculation, of statistics, of methods, timetables and routine; its practice is a science. Managers are necessary; leaders are essential. A good system will produce efficient managers, but more than that is needed. We must find managers who are not only skilled organizers but inspired and inspiring leaders, destined eventually to fill the highest ranks of control and direction. Such men will gather round them close-knit teams of subordinates like themselves and of technical experts whose efficiency, enthusiasm and loyalty will be unbeatable. Increasingly this is recognized and the search for leadership is on.

What should we look for? Where are we likely to find it? When we have found it, how shall we develop and use it? Can the experience of the army be any help? Let us see.

In this matter of leadership we in the Fighting Services have, of course, certainly very marked advantages over civil life:

- The principle of personal leadership is traditional and accepted.
- Besides, there is a strict legal code for the enforcement of obedience to lawful direction.
- Officers and men recognize that they are on the same side, fighting together against a common enemy.
- The commanders do not, in war at any rate, have to pay so much regard to the financial effects of their action.

I can well understand a businessman saying, 'If we had all that, management would indeed be simple!' So, lest you should think that military management is too easy, I would remind you that:

- Personal leadership exists only as long as the officers demonstrate it by superior courage, wider knowledge, quicker initiative and a greater readiness to accept responsibility than those they lead.
- Again, military command is not just a matter of shouting orders that will be obeyed for fear of punishment. Any commander's success comes more from being trusted than from being feared; from leading rather than driving.
- Officers and men feel themselves on the same side only as long as the officers, in all their dealings, show integrity and unselfishness and place the wellbeing of their men before their own.
- In war the general may not be haunted by finance, but his is the responsibility for good management and economy in matters more important than money – his men's lives.

These things, not stars and crowns or the director's Rolls-Royce, are the badges of leadership anywhere.

In industry you will never have to ask men to do the stark things demanded of soldiers, but the men you employ are the same men. Instead of rifles they handle tools; instead of guns they serve machines. They have changed their khaki and jungle-green for workshop overalls and civvies suits. But they are the same men and they will respond to leadership of the right kind as they have always done.

Infuse your management with leadership; then they will show their mettle in the workshop as they have on the battlefield. Like me, they would rather be led than managed. Wouldn't you?

WHO MAKES THE DIFFERENCE?

As a strategic leader you may hope that when members of
your top team do achieve their goals and say to themselves
in Lao Tzu's words, 'We did this ourselves', they will also
look towards you and add, 'But *you* made a difference.'

Strategic leaders are frequently invited to identify their
legacy – the difference or added value that should result
from their tenure of office. To leave an organization with
a large 'golden handshake', however it is termed, but to
leave it no better than when you came, does not count as
success in this book. It will be natural for you one day
to look back in hindsight and say to yourself, 'I made a
difference there in these specific ways . . .' Or, to put it
slightly differently, 'Had I not been there such-and-such
would not have happened.'

Actually, it doesn't matter too much if others recognize
that difference, still less that it is acknowledged in public.
Often you are the only person who knows the full story.
What stays with you forever is the knowledge of how you
did make a difference. It may or may not have led on to
other things – who can follow all the threads of destiny? –
but you played your part effectively and creatively.

But I don't want to leave you there. We are commanded
to love others as we love ourselves. If making a difference
matters so much to you, why not make it your business as a
strategic leader *to see that each individual in your organization
also has a sense of making a difference*? On the principle that
everyone finds time for what they see and feel to be important, you will not find difficulty in focusing upon it and
taking time to check that it is happening at other levels of
leadership as well.

Human Resources is a much-used phrase these days,

employed now as a substitute for the older (military) term *personnel*. It is a bit of management-speak really, for it appears to classify people as if they were economic resources, along with finance, machinery and energy. But it is a misuse of terms. For a human *resource* is not the available number of people to act as means at your disposal to achieve strategic ends. *Resource* indicates a *new* source of supply or support, one that may be hidden from view. The word itself comes from the Latin *resurgere*, to rise again. For example, you may not discover your own personal resources until you are confronted with an unexpected or threatening crisis in your life. Organizations are not dissimilar. The phrase *human resource* really describes that inner or hidden reserve of energy, life or spirit that lies within the human individual. Crisis, opportunity or ideals are usually the three keys that unlock it, and leaders are no more than catalysts in the process.

KEY POINTS: FINDING TIME FOR INDIVIDUALS

- 'Our costliest expenditure is time,' said the Greek philosopher Theophrastus (c. 370–287 B. C.), and how right he was. The potential time bill for a strategic leader – 'inside the egg' and beyond the bounds of the organization – is an enormous one. Two things are necessary: (1) to avoid wasting time on what should not concern you, and (2) to establish some clear priorities and policies as to how you are going to spend it.
- The ten principles of effective time management should be observed. Apart from learning to say no – the chief timesaver of all – the principle of delegation is critically important. To a person of above-average common sense, the candidates for delegation are usually fairly obvious.

Delegation saves you from becoming immersed in day-to-day administration or descending into too much detail. As a policy, if something can be delegated, delegate it.

- Don't just delegate the work that does not interest you. Delegating interesting and challenging work is a means of developing people. Remember, however, that delegation is not abdication, and you remain accountable: 'The buck stops here.'

- Apart from accountability (as contrasted with responsibility), you cannot delegate leadership. At strategic level that means spending your time on the seven functions of your role (see page 85). Time to *think* is top of that list, as strategy, you will recall – is the *thinking* appropriate to a leader-in-chief.

- Apart from strategic direction and building teamwork, the third circle in the trinity that focuses on the *individual* invites your attention and time. It was not so much neglected by the top managers of yesteryear; it simply did not appear on their mental screen.

- You should develop a friendly but professional one-to-one relationship with each member of your top team, different in each case but equal in favour. Functions of *planning, reviewing* and *informing* are the main items on the standing agenda of this ongoing two-way communication. Take opportunities to help your colleagues to grow as operational and strategic leaders. At least one of them should be in the running as your successor.

- That every individual person in the organization should make a difference is strategically important these days. Make it your business to see it happens.

- Each individual person needs to know the plot, to understand clearly their part in the drama, to be encouraged to put their whole selves into it, and – when the curtain goes down – to have an enduring sense that their contribution has been worthwhile. This will not happen unless you and your leader-colleagues demonstrate in practical ways that each individual member matters to you.

The task of leadership is not to put greatness into humanity,
but to elicit it, for the greatness is already there.

John Buchan, Scottish writer

CONCLUSION

THE WAY AHEAD

The author Graham Greene was once asked if he considered himself to be a great novelist. 'Not great,' he replied, 'but one of the best.'

If this book has aroused in you the desire to be 'one of the best' as a really effective strategic leader, I will rest my pen. If, moreover, you have found some practical ideas and suggestions that will take you on your way, I shall be delighted.

Beyond that I hope that somewhere you may have heard the inspiring music of leadership – 'good leadership and leadership for good.' Competencies, functions, models, checklists, action plans – all have their place in helping you to form a framework for effective strategic leadership, buttressed by the examples of those ahead of you on the journey. As effective leadership is now seen to be of such importance, it is natural that textbooks of the 'how-to-do-it' variety will appear. I have written some of them myself.

How far you can progress on the path to greatness as a strategic leader depends upon your natural ability, your opportunities and your willingness to learn. Why is continuous learning so important? Because it develops your *capability*. Two thousand years ago, Cicero said the same thing. He admitted the power of natural talent, but went on to say, 'When the method and discipline of knowledge are added to talent, *the result is usually altogether outstanding.*'

By developing your capability you are adding to your resources: the stock or reserve that you can draw on when necessary. Your ability to meet and handle situations is enhanced. In a word, you are becoming a more resourceful person.

'You cannot teach leadership, it can only be learned,' it has been wisely said. True, but it takes *continuous* learning throughout your career if you are to become 'one of the best'. May this introductory guide be for you the beginning – perhaps even your very first step – on the long journey that leads you to mastery in the art of strategic leadership. Nowhere in any of my books have I said that leadership is easy. But you will find nothing so personally rewarding or profitable to those fortunate enough to work with you.

There must be a beginning in any great matter, but the continuing unto the end until it be thoroughly finished yields the true glory.
Sir Francis Drake, Elizabethan sailor and navigator

INDEX

extracts reading groups
competitions books new
discounts extracts
competitions
books new
events
reading groups
events books
extracts
new titles reading groups
interviews
discounts
new books events
events new events
discounts extracts discounts
www.panmacmillan.com
extracts events reading groups
competitions books extracts new
books